nF418943

Also available by Kae R. Nelson

A Woman Named Dale: In the Shadows of Grace

(fiction)

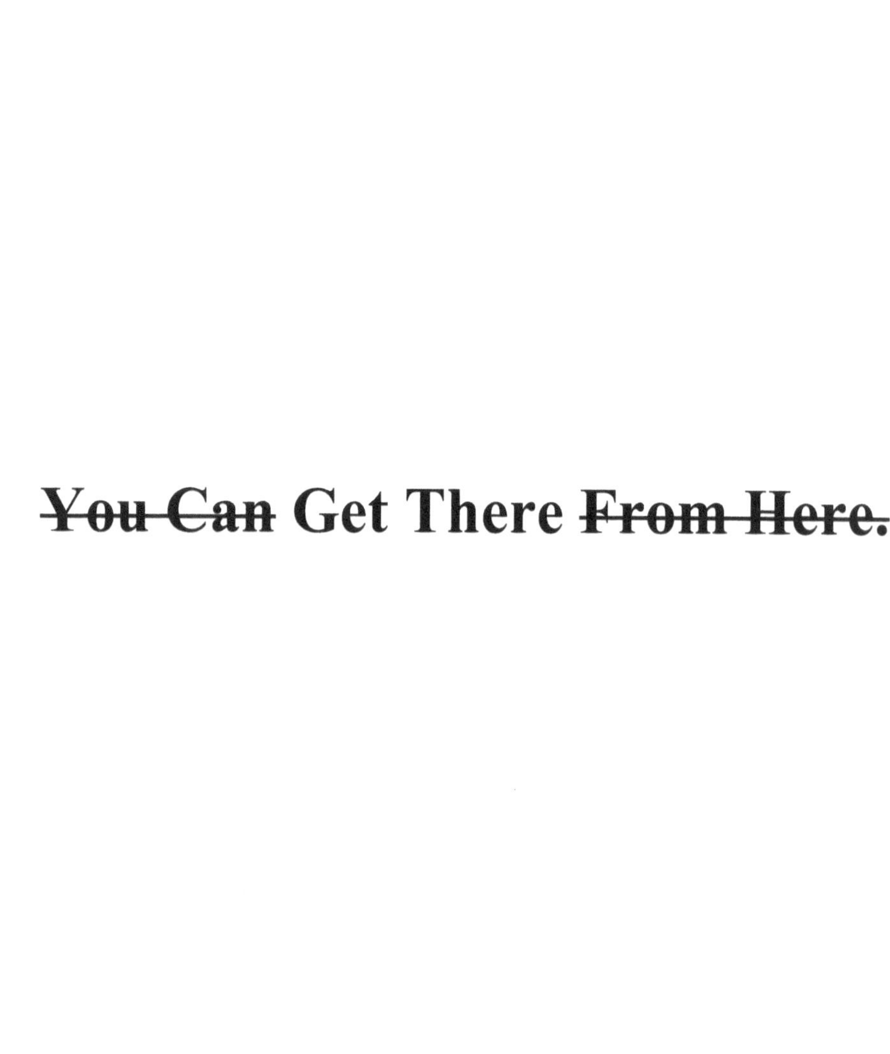

You Can Get There From Here.

~~You Can~~ Get There ~~From Here.~~
A No-excuses guide to showing up for yourself.

By: Kae R. Nelson

The Library of Congress Catalog-in-Publication data available upon request.

ISBN (paperback): 979-8-9994974-3-7

Cover design by Kae R. Nelson.
Printed and published in the United States.

www.kaernelson.com

Publication Date: March 20, 2026

First Edition: March 2026.
10 9 8 7 6 5 4 3 2 1

For you.

TABLE OF CONTENTS

INTRODUCTION
SO... I WROTE A SELF-HELP BOOK (YEAH, I KNOW)

You know what's wild? I never thought I'd write a self-help book. I mean, really. Me? A woman who's had to Google "how to stop overthinking everything" more times than I care to admit? A woman who gives herself pep talks in the car mirror and has full-blown motivational speeches with her reflection while brushing her teeth? A woman who's made peace with the fact that she talks to herself like she's hosting her own personal TED talk.

Yeah. That's me.

But here I am, writing it. Not because I think I've cracked the code to a perfect life (spoiler alert: I haven't), and not because I've discovered some magical formula that makes everything easy (if I had, trust me, I'd be sipping something tropical on a beach somewhere instead of sitting here with my laptop and a cold cup of coffee).

I'm writing this because I've lived a life where people loved to tell me what I couldn't do, couldn't have, and couldn't become. Too this, not enough that. Too Black for some spaces, not Black enough for others. Too loud, too quiet, too ambitious, too content, too much, not enough. You know the drill, somebody always has an opinion about how you should exist in the world.

And for a long time, I believed it. We all do, don't we? We start shapeshifting ourselves to fit into other people's comfort zones, trying to squeeze into boxes that were never meant for us anyway. We shrink ourselves to make others feel bigger, dim our light so others don't feel outshined, and apologize for taking up space in our own lives.

But somewhere along the way, I got tired of being smaller than I was. I got tired of waiting for permission to want what I wanted. I got tired of playing it safe and calling it wisdom. And most of all, I got tired of letting other people's limitations become my reality.
I believe you should too.

CHAPTER 1: THE CLIFFSNOTES VERSION OF ME

Let me give you the rundown: I'm a retired disabled veteran who spent years serving my country, which taught me things about resilience and purpose that no classroom ever could. I'm a high school English teacher, which means I spend my days convincing teenagers that grammar actually matters and that reading isn't a form of torture Some days are more successful than others.

I'm a wife who's learned that marriage is less about finding someone perfect and more about finding someone whose imperfections complement your own. I'm a mother who's discovered that raising humans is equal parts terrifying and amazing, and that most of the time you're just winging it and hoping for the best.

I'm a PhD candidate because apparently, I thought I needed more stress in my life, but really because I believe in the power of education and the importance of never stopping learning. I'm a child of God who's learned that faith isn't about having all the answers but about trusting the journey even when you can't see the destination.

I'm a writer who's always been fascinated by the power of words to heal, to challenge, to inspire, and to transform. I'm a reader who believes that books are portals to other worlds and other possibilities. And I'm someone who believes deeply in second chances, third chances, and as many chances as it takes to get it right. But most importantly, I'm someone who's learned that the only person who can change your life is you.

The Lists That Led Me Here

I've made a lot of lists in my life. So many lists. Grocery lists that I leave on the kitchen counter. "Things I'll start on Monday" lists that get pushed to the following Monday, and then the Monday after that. "Reasons why I should quit this job" lists. "What I want to accomplish before I die" lists that I write when I'm feeling particularly philosophical.

But none of those lists moved the needle like learning how to set real goals, not just wishes or dreams or someday-maybes, but actual, concrete, achievable goals with strategies and timelines and accountability that didn't rely on someone else dragging me across the finish line.

Don't get me wrong, I believe in support systems. I believe in prayer warriors and best friends who show up with snacks and reality checks. I believe in group chats that cheer you on and therapy that helps you untangle the knots in your mind. I believe in community and connection and the power of people who believe in you when you don't believe in yourself.

But, more important than all of that, is the power of learning to show up for yourself when no one else is watching. The power of being your own cheerleader, your own accountability partner, your own source of motivation. The power of getting up and doing the thing even when the room is silent and no one's applauding.

Why This Book Exists

I decided to write this book because I've had one too many conversations with brilliant, talented, amazing people who told me they were too old, too tired, too late, or too far gone to pursue their dreams. People who said they didn't start because they didn't have anyone to hold them accountable. People who were waiting for the perfect moment, the perfect circumstances, the perfect support system.

And I get it. Life is heavy. Life is complicated. Life has a way of throwing curveballs when you're expecting softballs. I've learned that waiting for perfect conditions is just another way of saying you're not going to start at all.

I want to teach you what I've learned about being your own motivation, your own accountability partner, your own biggest fan. I want to show you how to create plans that bend with the wind but don't break. Plans that absorb the chaos but still get you where you want to go. Plans that work in the real world, not just in the fantasy world where everything goes according to script.

Because chaos is coming. It always is. Life is going to life, as they say. But when you expect the unexpected, prepare for the detours, and stop acting like your success depends on everything going perfectly, that's when you start winning.

The Frustration That Fueled This

Was frustration part of my motivation for writing this? Absolutely. I was frustrated watching brilliant people stay stuck because they didn't know how capable they were. Seeing talented individuals shrink themselves because someone had convinced them they weren't worthy of their dreams. I was frustrated by the number of people who were letting their inner critic run the show while their authentic voice sat quietly in the corner.

But mostly, I was frustrated by the lies we told ourselves. The lie that it's too late, we're too broken, or that we need permission from others to pursue what matters to us. We do not have to wait until we feel ready, have enough experience, or the stars align perfectly.

Your self-doubt is often the loudest voice in the room, but it doesn't have to be the voice you listen to. Not the haters, not the critics, not even the people who side-eye you every time you try something new. Most of the time, you are the one telling yourself, "I can't." And it's time to have a conversation with that voice.

What You'll Find in These Pages

This book isn't about toxic positivity or pretending that mindset alone will solve all your problems. I am not going to give techniques to ignore the challenges you face or pretend that systemic inequalities don't exist. I am a veteran, but I am not going to tell you to pull yourself up by your bootstraps or any of that nonsense.

This book is about getting honest with yourself, your dreams, your fears, and what's really holding you back. We must all learn to distinguish between legitimate obstacles and our own limiting beliefs. I want to help you develop the skills you need to navigate challenges without being defeated by them.

We're going to talk about:

- Why it's never too late to start over or start something new
- How to stop letting your past define your future
- The power of consistency over perfection
- Why comparison is the thief of joy and how to break free from it
- How to get out of your feelings when they're keeping you stuck
- Why you don't need external validation to pursue your dreams
- How to identify and challenge the limiting beliefs that are running your life
- The importance of boundaries and how to set them without feeling guilty
- How to use self-reflection and planning to create your own roadmap

- Why failure isn't the opposite of success but part of it
- How to build confidence through action, not just positive thinking or affirmations
- Why your journey doesn't have to be perfect to be meaningful

Who This Book Is For

It's for the person who's been waiting for permission that's never coming. For the dreamer who's been told to be realistic, and the person who's made mistakes and thinks that it disqualifies them from happiness. Anyone who's ready to stop being their own worst enemy and start being their own best friend.

If you want practical strategies and not just inspiration, you've grabbed the right book. Let's do the work, even when it's uncomfortable. You deserve more than what you're currently experiencing.

A Note About Perfection

Before we dive in, I need to tell you I'm not perfect. This book isn't perfect, and your journey won't be perfect either. That's not just okay, that's the point.

I've made mistakes. I've failed at things. I've started projects I didn't finish, set goals I didn't reach, and made decisions I later regretted. I've been my own worst critic and my own biggest obstacle more times than I can count.

I've also learned that perfection isn't the goal. Progress is. Growth is. Learning to show up for your life even when it's messy and complicated and nothing like what you planned is the goal.

So, as you read this book, give yourself permission to be imperfect. Give yourself permission to take what serves you and leave what doesn't, as my friend S.D. would say. Give yourself permission to go at your own pace and make your own mistakes to find your own way.

Your Invitation

This book is my invitation to you. An invitation to stop waiting for someday and start now. Stop asking for permission and start giving it to yourself. Don't let fear make your decisions, but let your dreams guide your actions.

You can get there from here, wherever "there" is for you. Whether "there" is a new career, a healthier relationship with yourself or a creative project you've been putting off. You don't have to have it all figured out.

You just have to start.

Start right here, right now, with the decision to believe that you deserve more than you're currently experiencing and that you have the power to create it.

Let's Do This

So here we are, at the beginning of something new.

Your life is not an accident. Your dreams are not coincidental. The calling you feel to grow, to change, to become more is not random. That's your soul telling you that you're ready for the next chapter.

You can get there from here. I believe that with every fiber of my being. And by the time you finish this book, I hope you'll believe it too.

Let's get into it.

/

CHAPTER 2: THE MYTH OF "TOO LATE"

You are not too old, too behind, too late, or too much anything to do the thing sitting in your gut like a dream-shaped boulder. Society loves to sell us this imaginary deadline. They've got us believing that if we didn't achieve X by 25, or Y by 30, or have our life entirely figured out by the time we're out of diapers, we've somehow missed our shot. But who decided that? Instagram? Your aunt who reminds you about your "biological clock"? A fourth-grade teacher once said, "You're not leadership material"?

This chapter is for anyone who looked in the mirror and said, "I should've started sooner." You didn't. And yet, you're here. Breathing. Reading. Feeling that tug in your chest that maybe, just maybe, it's still possible. We're going to dismantle the myth that your chance has passed. We'll talk about ageism, fear, arbitrary life timelines, and introduce you to real people who made their dreams bloom on what others might've called "borrowed time."

Spoiler alert: they weren't borrowing anything, they owned it. And so do you.

Let's Get One Thing Straight: You're Not Too Late

Our world is obsessed with timelines. Graduate by 22. Be successful by 25. Married with kids by 30. If you miss a milestone, society starts handing out pity like Halloween candy, and not the good kind. The truth is dreams don't have expiration dates. There is no cut-off point for becoming who you were meant to be.

Still, so many of us walk around with a heavy ache that sounds like "I should have..."

"I should have started earlier."

"I should have known what I wanted by now."

"I should be further along."

Let's pause right here. Those "should haves" aren't even yours. They belong to the expectations of a society that doesn't know your story, battles, healing, or dreams.

So, let's rewrite the story, not with delusion, but with power.

The "I should have" mindset is one of the most subtle forms of self-punishment. It creeps in quietly, disguising itself as reflection, but it's rumination in costume. It doesn't ask you to grow. It demands you to relive. Over and over again.

"I should have stayed in school."

"I should have pursued that dream harder."

"I should have known better."

It's a trap. A mental loop that positions regret as your guide and drowns out everything you've survived, built, or become since.

Hindsight will always know more than you, friend. Of course, you could have chosen differently. But the person you are today only exist because of the exact road you took including the detours, breakdowns, and the exits you weren't supposed to take but did anyway. Even in your hardheadedness, when you didn't listen to God when He told you to do something you didn't want. You messed around and found out.

So instead of sitting ashamed of "I should have," start asking better questions:

"What did I learn from that season?"

"What part of me grew in that hard place?"

"What does healing and growth look like today, not yesterday?"

"How can I honor that version of me without being imprisoned by those choices?"

The past is a teacher not a prison. It was never meant to lock you in, just to shape how you walk forward.

You are not a failed dream.

You are a living, breathing reroute.

You are allowed to grow in ways that don't fit your original script.

The next chapter doesn't have to look like the first one.

It just has to be yours.

The Stage I Didn't Stand On

I graduated from high school in 2005, loud in spirit but unsure in path. What I did know was that I was destined to be someone special, not necessarily famous, but impactful. I wasn't aiming for red carpets; I just wanted to matter. I was the weird theater kid, a mask ready for every occasion, with low self-esteem and a brain that ran on stories and scenes. Theater didn't just accept my weirdness, it applauded it.

My high school theater teacher, Mr. Ipina, was one of my first true allies. He wasn't just a teacher. He was a friend, a mentor, a mirror. He let me cry, vent, dream big, and be fully, eccentrically me. Sure, I could act, sing, and build a set, but my real magic? Stage management. I memorized everyone's lines, tracked cues like a hawk, built sets from dreams, and ran productions like a general with paint on her boots.

One day, preparing for a one-act play competition, we were trying to load a single box truck with all our gear. This was in the south, early 2000s. Sports were more important than the arts, so we had to raise funds to get even one truck. It was chaos. Frustration. Disbelief. No one thought it could fit. Not only could we not afford a second truck, but it was too late to get one.

I watched quietly, then said, "Let me try." And like a sweaty game of real-life Tetris, I did it. Every prop, every set piece, every costume—perfectly packed. The door closed with barely an inch to spare. Mr. Ipina laughed, "She's playing Tetris!" That moment sealed it for me. All things theatre was going to be my life.

My friends dreamed of Broadway. I promised I'd be their stage manager, keeping everything upright behind the scenes. But life, as it often does, had other plans. I went straight to college, double majoring in English and Theatre. I was 19, newly married, and determined to keep my promise. But real-life crept in. Bills, jobs that didn't pay enough, and a world that didn't know what to do with a small-town stage manager with no real credits. I worked at Subway. I worked at Convergys. I worked at staying afloat. And at 21, I joined the military. And just like that, my path split.

I still took classes while I served, but a theatre degree doesn't translate to online coursework in a war zone. My friends kept going. They earned roles, recognition, and momentum. I deployed, trained, bled, and survived, but a part of me grieved. I thought I had failed because Broadway would never know my name. I hated myself for allowing my dream to die somewhere in basic training. I believed I would never be as good at anything. I believed that for years.

While I wore my uniform with pride, inside I felt...less. Like my dreams had expired. I wasn't on stage. I wasn't behind one either. Yeah, we called deployment locations "theatres," but that is the only similarity. I compared my journey to theirs, my classmates chasing curtain calls while I chased security protocols. The military uses "theatre" to describe a geographic area where military operations and campaigns happened. It's a large-scale zone, including land, sea, and air, where strategy, survival, and sometimes sacrifice unfolded.

But that wasn't the kind of theater I loved. The military's "theatre" didn't offer scripts or rehearsals. It didn't let me slip into a character or feel the pulse of the crowd. It wasn't the kind of pretend that gave me freedom. I missed being that high school kid, in love with the game of make-believe, where the stage allowed me to escape real life, even for a moment.

I often beat myself up with "I should haves."
I should've done better.
I should've stayed.
I should've tried harder.

It took me over a decade, at a duty station in Anchorage, Alaska, for that shame to finally melt. I woke up one day and realized how cruelly I'd been holding myself hostage to "should haves." I thought I missed the train all those years, but I'd been building an entirely different vehicle made of resilience, courage, adaptability, and strength.

What I Learned From That Season

I learned that dreams could evolve, and detours don't mean defeat. That season taught me resilience, self-reliance, and how to lead from the background, even if the background looked more like a battlefield than a stage. I learned how to adapt and survive while still carrying the core of who I was. Real-life improv.

My strength grew. My discipline and courage matured. I developed a quiet confidence that didn't need applause to validate its worth. While I wasn't on a literal stage, I became a powerful director of my survival, and the survival of others, commanding chaos with grace.

What My Healing and Growth Look Like Today

Today, healing looks like no longer punishing myself for missed opportunities. Growth looks like recognizing that the life I built is meaningful, worthy, and impactful. It means honoring my military path as not a failure of my dream but as the foundation for a new, broader one.

How I Honor That Version of Me Without Being Imprisoned by Their Choices

I honor her by acknowledging her bravery, her hope, and her hustle. She did her best with what she knew. I don't need to carry her regrets, but I can carry her lessons. I give her grace, not grief. Her choices led me here, and here is worthy.

If you're reading this and you're holding on to your own "I should've" story, don't. Don't let a past version of your dream invalidate the life you've built. Don't punish yourself for detours. The version of you who chased one dream built the version of you who can now chase another. And maybe the path you're on now is richer, deeper, and more powerful than the one you thought you missed. Don't let the "should haves" be the reason your journey stalls. They don't own your story. You do.

Ageism, Fear & The Timeline Trap

Ageism is sneaky. It tells you your best days are behind you. That success is a young person's game and reinvention is embarrassing.

But look around.

Toni Morrison published her first novel at 39. Vera Wang entered fashion at 40. Samuel L. Jackson got his breakout role at 46. Colonel Sanders franchised KFC at 62. Laura Ingalls Wilder published her first "Little House" book at 65. Nola Ochs earned her college degree at 95. Kimani Maruge enrolled in primary school at 84 and became the world's oldest elementary school student. Grandma Moses began painting seriously in her late 70s. Peter Mark Roget invented the thesaurus at 73.

The fear that you've missed your chance or you're too old is a lie dressed in panic. You're exactly where you need to be to start. Right now. Today.

What ageism never accounts for is depth. With age comes a richness of lived experience that no 20-year-old prodigy can replicate. It's not about dismissing youth, it's about honoring the value of life lived. Every scar, every pivot, every chapter of survival gives your work, your voice, and your vision a wisdom that's earned, not taught. When people call it "starting over," remind them you're not starting from scratch, but from experience.

We don't question flowers that bloom in late spring. We don't shame trees that take longer to bear fruit. Why, then, do we shame ourselves for blossoming on a different timeline? Our culture is obsessed with youth, but some of the most profound revolutions personally and publicly are led by people who've lived long enough to know exactly who they are and what they stand for. That's not failure. That's power.

Let's normalize changing our minds, pursuing new dreams, or reigniting old ones at any age. Let's stop pretending there's a "too late" and start celebrating the bravery it takes to begin again. There is no expiration date on purpose. If you're breathing, your story is still being written. And some of the best chapters come after the world said it was over.

Late Bloomers Aren't Late. They're Just on Time.

The concept of being a "late bloomer" assumes there's a universal schedule for success, fulfillment, and achievement. But who wrote that schedule? Who decided that creativity peaks at 25, that career changes after 40 are desperate moves, or that starting a family, a business, or a new passion after a certain age is somehow less valid than doing it earlier?

The truth is, some of us need more time to become who we're meant to be. Some of us need to live through certain experiences, face specific challenges, or heal from wounds before we're ready to step into our purpose. Some of us need to try other paths first, not because we're lost, but because those paths are teaching us something essential about ourselves.

Consider the oak tree and the bamboo. Bamboo can grow up to three feet in a single day once it starts, but it spends years developing its root system underground before any growth is visible. The oak tree grows slowly and steadily, taking decades to reach its full majesty. Both are magnificent in their own time. Both serve their purpose. Neither is late.

Your timeline is sacred. The years you spent in other careers, other relationships, other versions of yourself weren't wasted. They were preparation. Every job that felt wrong was teaching you what felt right. Every relationship that didn't work was showing you what you needed. Every dream you abandoned was making space for the dream that would fit.

The woman who starts medical school at 45 brings a maturity and life experience that her 22-year-old classmates don't have. The man who opens his first restaurant at 55 has decades of understanding about service, quality, and what people really want. The person who writes their first novel at 60 has lived enough stories to tell one that matters.

We live in a culture that celebrates the young entrepreneur, the child prodigy, the overnight success. But we rarely talk about the beauty of the slow burn, the power of the long game, the wisdom that comes with time. We don't celebrate the courage it takes to start something new when you're supposed to have it all figured out already.

Some dreams are worth waiting for. Some purposes require seasoning. Some callings demand that you live a little, hurt a little, learn a little before you're ready to answer them.

If you're reading this and thinking you're behind, let me reframe that for you. You're not behind, you're building. You're not late, you're learning. You're not too old, you're experienced. You're not starting over; you're starting with everything you've learned so far. Change your perspective.

The world needs what you have to offer, and it needs it now, at this age, with this experience, in this season of your life. Your perspective is unique because of the path you've taken, not despite it.

The Danger of Comparison and Societal Pressure

Social media has turned everyone's highlight reel into your measuring stick. You see the 25-year-old CEO, the 30-year-old bestselling author, the 35-year-old who seems to have it all figured out, and you think you're failing. But you're comparing your behind-the-scenes to their highlight reel. You're comparing your chapter three to their chapter twenty.

What you don't see in those perfectly curated posts are the struggle, the failures, the support systems, the privileges, the luck, the timing that contributed to their success. You don't see the mental health struggles, the relationship sacrifices, the sleepless nights, the moments of doubt. You see the victory lap, not the race.

And even if their journey was as smooth as it appears, so what? Their timeline has nothing to do with yours. Their success doesn't diminish your potential. Their early start doesn't make your later start less valid.

The pressure to achieve at certain ages is largely artificial, created by a society that values productivity over humanity, speed over depth, youth over wisdom. But life isn't a race where everyone starts at the same line and runs the same course. We all start from different places, with different resources, different challenges, different gifts. Some of us are running marathons while others are running sprints. Some of us are climbing mountains while others are swimming in oceans.

The only timeline that matters is yours. The only useful comparison is between who you were yesterday and who you are today. The only pressure that's productive is the push you give yourself to keep growing, keep trying, keep becoming.

Society will always have opinions about what you should be doing and when you should be doing it. But society doesn't have to live your life. Society doesn't have to face your mirror. Society doesn't have to answer for your choices. You do.

So, stop letting society's timeline dictate your worth. Stop letting other people's journeys make you feel bad about your own. Stop apologizing for taking the scenic route, for changing directions, for starting later than expected.

Your path is yours. Your timing is yours. Your story is yours.

Recognizing and Dismantling Limiting Beliefs

The voice that tells you it's too late is not your intuition, it's your conditioning. It's the accumulation of every message you've received about age, success, and timing. It's the internalized ageism, the absorbed expectations, the inherited fears of a culture that worships youth and speed. But beliefs are not facts. They're just thoughts you've thought so many times they feel true. And if you can learn a limiting belief, you can unlearn it.

Start by noticing the stories you tell yourself about age and timing. Do you catch yourself thinking things like "I'm too old to start over," "I should have figured this out by now," or "It's too late for me?" These are beliefs, not truths.

Challenge these beliefs by asking yourself: Where did this belief come from? Is it actually true? What evidence do I have that contradicts this belief? What would I tell a friend who expressed this same limiting belief?

Replace limiting beliefs with empowering ones. Instead of "I'm too old," try "I'm experienced." Instead of "I'm behind," try "I'm on my own timeline." Instead of "It's too late," try "It's exactly the right time."

Surround yourself with stories that contradict your limiting beliefs. Read about people who started later and succeeded. Follow accounts that celebrate diverse timelines. Seek out communities that support non-traditional paths.

Remember that your beliefs shape your reality. If you believe it's too late, you'll look for evidence that supports that belief and miss opportunities that contradict it. If you believe you're exactly where you need to be, you'll approach your life with curiosity and possibility instead of regret and resignation.

The most powerful thing you can do is decide that your story isn't over. That your best chapters might still be ahead of you. That your dreams don't have expiration dates. That you're not too late, you're right on time.

The Power of Starting Where You Are

You don't have to have it all figured out to start. You don't have to be young to begin or be perfect to take the first step. You just have to be willing.

Starting where you are means accepting that you might not have as much time as someone younger, but you have something they don't: experience, wisdom, clarity about what matters, and often, fewer distractions. You know who you are in a way that younger people are still discovering. You know what you don't want, which is just as valuable as knowing what you do want.

Starting where you are means using your current resources, connections, and knowledge as steppingstones. The skills you developed in your previous career might be exactly what you need in your new venture. The network you built in one industry might open doors in another. The life experience you've gained might be the unique perspective that sets you apart.

Starting where you are means giving yourself permission to be a beginner again. Yes, it might feel uncomfortable to not be the expert in the room. Yes, it might be humbling to start at the bottom of a new field. But there's also something liberating about being a student again, about having room to grow, about not having to maintain an image of having it all together.

The most successful late starters are those who embrace their beginner's mind while leveraging their life experience. They're humble enough to learn but confident enough to contribute. They're open to new ways of doing things but grounded in their values and wisdom.

Your Dreams Don't Have Expiration Dates

Your dreams are not milk. They don't go bad after a certain date. They don't become less valid because you didn't pursue them in your twenties. They don't lose their power because you took a detour or ten.

Dreams evolve, but they don't expire. The dream you have at 45 might be different from the one you had at 25, but it's no less important. It might be more refined, more realistic, more aligned with who you've become. It might be informed by experience, tempered by wisdom, and strengthened by everything you've learned along the way.

Sometimes we need to live other lives before we're ready for our real life. Sometimes we need to try other dreams before we find the one that fits. Sometimes we need to become certain people before we're ready for certain purposes.

The dream you're carrying now, the one that feels too late, too ambitious, too risky might be exactly the right dream for exactly who you are right now. It might require the experience you've gained, or the skills you've developed. It might be a dream that could only be fulfilled by someone who has lived your life.

Don't let the myth of "too late" rob you of the dream that's meant for this season of your life. Don't let society's timeline dictate your possibilities. Don't let fear of starting over keep you from starting at all.

Your dreams are waiting for you. They've been patient while you lived other chapters, learned other lessons, became the person who could fulfill them. They're not going anywhere. They're not getting stale. They're getting ready.
And so are you.

You are not too old, too behind, too late, or too anything to pursue what matters to you. You are exactly the right age, with exactly the right experience, at exactly the right time to begin again.

Your timeline is not society's timeline. Your journey is not anyone else's journey. Your dreams are not bound by arbitrary deadlines or cultural expectations. They're bound only by your willingness to pursue them.

The world needs what you have to offer. It needs your perspective, your experience, your unique combination of skills and wisdom. It needs the book only you can write, the business only you can start, the art only you can create, the impact only you can make.

X

CHAPTER 3: LET'S TALK ABOUT YOUR INNER HATER (YES, YOU HAVE ONE)

You know that voice, don't you? The one that shows up right when you're about to hit "send" on that job application, raise your hand in the meeting, or step into something that scares you. It whispers that you're not good enough, smart enough, or deserving enough. That you're too much of this or not enough of that.

Meet your inner critic. And yes, you absolutely have one, even if you've convinced yourself you don't.

This voice isn't your friend, your protector, or your voice of reason, no matter how it disguises itself. It's your fear wearing a mask of logic, your past disappointments cosplaying as wisdom. It's the accumulated noise of every doubt, every harsh word, every time someone made you feel small rolled into one persistent, toxic narrator that lives rent-free in your head.

Your inner critic is not the boss. It doesn't get to write your story, and it definitely doesn't get to decide what you're capable of.

Understanding Your Inner Critic and How It Sabotages Your Dreams

Your inner critic is a master of disguise. It rarely shows up twirling its mustache like a cartoon villain. Instead, it poses as the voice of reason, whispering things like:

"Be realistic." "Don't get your hopes up." "Who do you think you are?" "You're not qualified for that." "People like us don't do things like that."

Sound familiar?

This voice didn't appear out of nowhere. It's been carefully constructed over years, built from the bricks of criticism, rejection, and fear. Maybe it sounds like your mother's worry, your father's doubt, or that teacher who told you to be more realistic about your future. Maybe it echoes the kids who laughed at your dreams or the boss who made you feel invisible.

The inner critic thinks it's protecting you. In its twisted logic, if it can convince you not to try, you can't fail. If it keeps you small, you won't get hurt. If it meets your expectations, you won't be disappointed.

But protection that keeps you from living isn't protection, it's prison.

Your inner critic doesn't just affect your confidence; it shapes your choices. It's the reason you don't speak up in meetings, apply for that promotion, start that business, or chase that dream. It's why you stay in relationships that don't serve you, jobs that drain you, and lives that feel too small.

Over time, if left unchecked, your inner critic doesn't just whisper suggestions, it starts giving orders. It dictates which opportunities you pursue, what rooms you enter, how loudly you speak, and how much space you allow yourself to take up. It creates a life of hesitation, perfectionism, and procrastination, convincing you that safety is better than growth and that being invisible is better than being vulnerable.

Understand that your inner critic is not your intuition. It's not your wisdom. It's not even your voice. It's fear dressed up in familiar clothing, and it's time to stop letting it drive.

Whose Voice Is That, Really?

Take a moment and listen to your inner critic. Whose voice does it sound like? Whose words is it using? Whose fear is it echoing?

I'll bet it's not even originally yours.

Most of our harshest internal voices are hand-me-downs. They're the echoes of people who spoke into our lives when we were too young, too trusting, or too vulnerable to know we didn't have to internalize their doubts as truth.

Maybe it's your mother's anxiety about money, so now you tell yourself you're "not good with finances" every time you think about starting a business.

Maybe it's your father's belief that creativity doesn't pay bills, so now you dismiss your artistic dreams as "impractical."

It could be a teacher who told you that you weren't "college material," and now you question your intelligence every time you're in a room with educated people.

Maybe it's an ex who convinced you that you were "too much" or "not enough," and now you shrink yourself in every relationship.

These voices became yours because you heard them during formative moments. But just because you've carried them doesn't mean you have to keep them. Just because they've been with you for years doesn't mean they belong to you.

It's time to give them back.

When you catch your inner critic in action, ask yourself: "Who said this to me first?" Then remind yourself: "That was their limitation, not mine. That was their fear, not my truth. That was their story, not my reality."

You get to choose which voices you listen to. You get to decide which thoughts get real estate in your mind. You get to evict the voices that don't serve your growth, your peace, or your purpose.

The Real Cost of Listening to Your Inner Hater

Let's be honest about what your inner critic is costing you.

It's not just confidence, though it steals that. It's not just opportunities, though it blocks plenty of those too. The real cost of your inner critic is your life. The life you could be living if you weren't spending so much energy fighting a voice in your head.

Think about all the times you've:

- Stayed quiet when you had something valuable to say.
- Declined opportunities because you "weren't ready."
- Played small to make others comfortable.
- Apologized for taking up space
- Dimmed your light so others wouldn't feel threatened.
- Stayed in situations that didn't serve you because change felt too risky.
- Convinced yourself you were being "realistic" when you were really being afraid.

Every time you listen to your inner critic, you're choosing fear over growth, safety over possibility, or comfort over calling. You're trading your dreams for the illusion of protection, and that protection isn't even real. Your inner critic can't protect you from failure, rejection, or disappointment. Life will hand you those experiences regardless. All your inner critic can do is ensure that when difficult things happen, you'll also have the added weight of regret, and the knowledge that you didn't even try.

Your inner critic promises safety but delivers stagnation. It promises protection but delivers prison.

Five Steps to Identify, Confront, and Silence Your Inner Critic

1. Catch It in the Act

You can't fight what you can't see. The first step is developing awareness of when your inner critic shows up and what triggers its appearance.

Start paying attention to the voice in your head. Notice when it gets louder, harsher, more persistent. Is it when you're about to try something new? When you're feeling vulnerable? When you're around certain people or in specific situations?

Keep track of the patterns. Notice the language it uses, the tone it takes, the timing of its attacks. The more conscious you become of your inner critic's habits, the less power it has to operate in the shadows.

When you catch it, name it. "Oh, there's my inner critic again." This simple act of naming creates distance between you and the voice. It reminds you that you are not your thoughts, you are the observer of your thoughts. And observers have choice.

2. Challenge the Narrative

Your inner critic speaks in absolutes. "You always mess up." "You never get it right." "No one will take you seriously." These statements feel true because they're delivered with such conviction, but conviction doesn't equal accuracy.

When your inner critic starts its monologue, interrupt it with questions:

- "Is this actually true, or is this fear talking?"
- "What evidence do I have that contradicts this statement?"
- "Would I say this to someone I love?"
- "Is this thought helping me grow or keeping me stuck?"
- "What would I tell my best friend if they said this about themselves?"

Demand receipts from your inner critic. Make it prove its claims with concrete evidence. Most of the time, you'll find that your inner critic is long on drama and short on facts.

3. Talk Back (And Don't Be Polite About It)

I'm a professional at talking back to my inner critic. Some people might think it makes me a little crazy, but I'd rather be crazy than controlled by fear.

I don't wait for my inner critic to finish its dissertation on why I'm not enough. I jump right in with responses like:

- "That's not true."
- "Not today, Satan."
- "Thanks for your input, but I didn't ask."
- "I've heard this story before, and I'm not buying it."
- "The devil is a liar, and the truth ain't in him."

On days when my voice feels too quiet to fight back, I lean on my support system. My husband has become a master at recognizing when my inner critic is winning and steps in with truth when I can't find my own.

Talking back isn't about ego but survival. It's about refusing to let fear have the final word in your story. You don't have to be polite to thoughts that are trying to diminish you. Sometimes you must meet your inner critic with a full chest and a firm voice.

4. Rewrite the Script

Replace those toxic thoughts with empowering truths. This isn't about lying to yourself or pretending problems don't exist, it's about speaking to yourself with the same compassion you'd show someone you love.

Instead of "I'm not ready," try "I'm learning and growing." Instead of "I don't belong here," try "I deserve to be here as much as anyone else." Instead of "I always mess up," try "I'm human, and humans make mistakes while learning." Instead of "I'm too old/young/inexperienced," try "I bring a unique perspective that adds value."

The goal isn't to eliminate all critical thinking, it's to eliminate destructive thinking. There's a difference between honest assessment and self-attack. Learn to critique your actions without condemning your worth.

5. Get the Right Kind of Support

If you want someone to gently tiptoe around your feelings and tell you only what you want to hear, this step will be challenging. Real support doesn't come from people who will baby you, it comes from people who love you enough to tell you the truth.

Whether through therapy, coaching, or trusted relationships, you need people in your corner who can help you distinguish between your authentic voice and the voice of your inner critic. You need people who will call out your self-limiting beliefs with love but without compromise. If they won't tell you that there is a booger in your nose, they are not the right person.

The right support person will say things like:

- "That's your fear talking, not your wisdom."
- "You're being harder on yourself than the situation warrants."
- "What evidence do you have for that belief?"
- "Who lied to you?"

This kind of honest feedback helps you break free from the prison of your own mind. It holds up a mirror so you can see when your inner critic is running the show. It reminds you of your strength when you've forgotten your own power.

Building Self-Compassion and Unshakeable Confidence

Building self-compassion isn't about lowering standards or accepting mediocrity. It's about learning to treat yourself with the same kindness you'd show someone else. You should speak to yourself in ways that motivate rather than devastate, that inspire growth rather than inspire shame.

Speak to Yourself Like Someone You Love

This lesson hit me hard because I used to pride myself on being blunt. I called it "real." I'd say, "I'm diabetic, I don't sugar-coat anything," and people would laugh. But over time, I realized there's a difference between honesty and harm, between being direct and being destructive.

I had to learn that truth delivered without compassion often misses its mark entirely. Would I say this to someone I care about? Would I say it this way? The answer was usually no.

Speaking to yourself with love doesn't mean lying or avoiding accountability. It means delivering truth wrapped in grace. It means being as patient with your learning process as you would be with anyone else's.

Create Your Own "Atta Girl/Boy" Book

I learned this from my Uncle Otis, who served in my home town's police force for nearly 30 years. Through decades of witnessing humanity at its worst, he found a way to protect his peace and perspective. He kept what he called his "Attaboy Book." This is a collection of notes, commendations, thank-you cards, and reminders of the good he was doing in the world.

When the job got heavy or the criticism was too loud (both external and internal), he'd pull out that book. It was his evidence that he was making a difference, that his work mattered, that he was enough.

Inspired by him, I keep my own version. I screenshot compliments, save encouraging emails, and document moments of progress I might otherwise brush off. These are my receipts that I am enough. I'm growing and contributing, even when it doesn't feel like it.

Start your own collection today. It doesn't need to be fancy. It can be a notebook, a folder on your phone, or a jar on your dresser. The goal is to have a place where your wins live, ready to remind you of your worth when your inner critic tries to convince you otherwise.

Practice Self-Compassion, Not Perfection

You will mess up. You will have bad days. You will make mistakes, say the wrong thing, miss opportunities, piss people off, and fall short of your own expectations. This doesn't make you a failure, it makes you human.

The goal isn't to become perfect but to become kind. Kind to yourself in your struggles, patient with yourself in your learning, and gentle with yourself in your growth.

Self-compassion isn't self-indulgence, it's self-preservation. It's the foundation that allows you to take risks, make mistakes, and keep going anyway.

Use Affirmations That Actually Mean Something

Let me be clear: I'm not talking about magical thinking or manifestation. I'm not suggesting you can simply speak something into existence, with no action, and watch it materialize. That's not my ministry.

When I look at the amazing things that have happened in my life, I take no credit. That's God. The way He has shown up, covered me, and carried me through things I didn't think I'd survive, no affirmation could have ever manufactured that. That was divine intervention.

But there's a difference between magical thinking and truthful self-talk. I'm talking about affirmations that are rooted, that speak to who you're becoming, that remind you of what's actually true about you.

Things like:

- "I'm allowed to take up space."
- "I can be both learning and worthy at the same time."
- "My past does not cancel my purpose."
- "It's okay to be proud of how far I've come."
- "I'm not perfect, but I am making progress."
- "I deserve the same compassion I give others."

These affirmations aren't about pretending you don't struggle, they're about remembering that you're more than your struggles. They speak to the part of you that's trying, not the part that's convinced you've already failed.

Create affirmations that speak to your real life, your actual challenges, your genuine growth. Write them down, say them out loud, stick them where you'll see them. You don't have to believe them completely yet, just believe they're possible.

A Real-Life Battle with My Inner Critic

Let me tell you about the day my inner critic almost cost me my entire military career and how one act of courage changed everything.

I was nearing the end of my first enlistment in the USAF, stationed at Nellis AFB, NV, facing separation from the military because I didn't have a CJR—a Career Job Reservation and, to reenlist, I had to get a document signed. Without that signature, my military career would be over. The deadline was Monday. It was Saturday. No officers were around.

My husband and I were living paycheck to paycheck. We had grass growing through the cracks on our dining room floor. When we applied for government assistance, they told us we made $20 too much to qualify. Twenty dollars. I don't know where they saw that money, because we were barely surviving.

As I sat in my car after another failed attempt to find help, my inner critic showed up with a megaphone:

"You should have planned better." "You don't belong in the military anyway." "This is just confirmation that you're not good enough." "No one is going to help you. Just give up."

I called my husband, tears streaming, ready to surrender. But he stayed calm. He reminded me that we'd figure it out somehow. His faith gave me just enough strength to try one more time.

I went back to the Military Personnel Flight, walking the halls like a woman possessed, looking for any officer who might help. Every face I passed was enlisted.

My inner critic was having a field day:

"See? I told you this was hopeless." "You were foolish to even try." "This place doesn't want you."

I was turning to leave when I saw someone walk out of an office. As I do when I see anyone in uniform, I checked his rank. Officer.

Now, I almost let him walk right by. It was Saturday, probably his day off. Military folks guard their off time like treasure, and I didn't want to be a bother. My inner critic was cheering: "Let him go. You've embarrassed yourself enough." "You're gonna be a burden."

But something deeper, desperation mixed with divine intervention, opened my mouth and made me call out to him.

I told him my story, holding onto my military bearing like my life depended on it while tears threatened to spill over. He listened, looked at the paper, and then did something that threw me off completely, he smiled. My inner critic immediately interpreted this as mockery: "He's laughing at you. He's not going to help. This is humiliating." "No one cares." "You're pathetic."

But do you know what happened? He signed it. Right there in the hallway against the wall. He signed my document and changed the trajectory of my life. Then, he told me he wasn't supposed to come that day.

That officer may never know it, but he didn't just save my career, but he helped me realize that my inner critic is a liar. It had almost convinced me to give up when victory was literally one conversation away.

The lesson? Your inner critic is loudest when you're closest to breakthrough. It knows that courage is contagious, that one act of bravery can silence years of doubt. Don't let it win when you're inches from the finish line.

When I called my husband with the good news, the relief and pride in his voice reminded me why I fought. Why I don't give up. Why I refuse to let my inner critic write the end of my story. The fact that I'd brought peace to him was another boost.

To this day, my husband tells this story to our children. Not to put me on a pedestal, but to show them How good God is, the power of persistence, and how we all need to put in work not just words. To teach them that when life pushes hard, you must push back with presence. Just with one more try. Luke 11:5-10.

Your Inner Critic vs. Your Inner Truth

Your inner critic will always have something to say. It will always find reasons why you should wait, play small, or give up. But you also have another voice. It's your inner truth. It's quieter sometimes, especially when fear is loud, but it's always there.

Your inner truth is the voice that whispers "what if?" when your inner critic screams "impossible." It's the voice that says, "try again" when your inner critic says "give up." It's the voice that reminds you of your dreams when your inner critic lists your limitations.

Learning to distinguish between these voices is one of the most important skills you'll ever develop. One voice keeps you stuck; the other sets you free. One voice focuses on problems; the other finds possibilities. One voice rehearses your failures; the other recalls your resilience.

The more you listen to your inner truth, the stronger it becomes. The more you act on its guidance, the quieter your inner critic gets. Not silent, it may never be completely silent, but manageable. Ignorable. Powerless.

You're capable of more than you realize. You're stronger than your fears. You're worthier than your doubts, and you're allowed to take up as much space as your dreams require.

Taking Back Your Power

Your inner critic has been running the show for too long. It's time to fire it from its management position and put your authentic self back in charge.

This doesn't mean you'll never doubt yourself again or that fear will disappear entirely. It means you refuse to let doubt and fear make your decisions for you. It means you choose courage over comfort, growth over safety, and truth over the lies your inner critic tells.

Every time you talk back to your inner critic, you reclaim a piece of your power. Every time you choose to try despite your fear, you build evidence of your own strength. Every time you speak to yourself with compassion instead of criticism, you heal a part of your soul that's been wounded by harsh words.

Your dreams need a protector, not a saboteur. Your goals need a cheerleader, not a critic. Your growth needs encouragement, not enemy fire.

You are that protector. You are that cheerleader. You are the source of the encouragement you've been waiting for.

Your inner critic has had its say. Now it's time for your inner truth to take the mic. And when it does, the whole world will hear what you're capable of.

$\rightarrow$

CHAPTER 4: GOAL SETTING FOR THE REST OF US

I'll say it first: Traditional goal setting feels like a trap designed by people who've never had a bad day.

You know the drill. "Dream big but be realistic." "Success comes from structure." "Just follow the formula." Meanwhile, you're over here trying to find clean socks, manage your anxiety, keep your kids alive, pay the bills, and maybe carve out five minutes to think about what you want from life.

Traditional goal setting methods make multiple assumptions. They assume everyone starts at the same place, with the same resources, energy levels, and life circumstances. They assume you wake up every morning with laser focus, unlimited motivation, and a perfectly organized calendar. They assume your biggest obstacle is lack of clarity, not lack of childcare. They assume you need more structure, not more grace.

But what if you're building dreams while juggling major depression? What if you're chasing goals while healing from trauma? What if you're trying to grow while caring for aging parents, working two jobs, or just trying to keep your head above water?

This chapter is for the rest of us. The ones whose lives don't fit into neat, predictable boxes. The ones who need goal setting with room for chaos, strategies that bend without breaking, and permission to succeed imperfectly.

This isn't about chasing a perfect picture finish line. It's about making meaningful progress that honors where you are right now. Think of it as goal setting with grace, grit, and plenty of room for the beautiful, messy middle.

Why Traditional Goal Setting Falls Short

Traditional goal setting was designed for a world that doesn't exist. A world where everyone has the same advantages, the same mental health, the same family support, and the same 24 hours in a day.

But the reality is that some of us are running marathons while others are sprinting. Some of us are climbing mountains while others are swimming upstream. Some of us are building while others are rebuilding. Some of us are creating while others are healing.

Traditional goal setting frameworks don't account for this reality. They make success seem like a simple equation.

Clear goal + consistent action + enough time + motivation/affirmations = guaranteed results. But life isn't a second grade math problem. It's messy, unpredictable, and full of variables that can't be controlled or calculated.

When you're dealing with mental health challenges, traditional goal setting can feel impossible. Depression doesn't care about your 90-day plan. Anxiety doesn't respect your carefully crafted timeline. PTSD doesn't follow your productivity schedule.

When you're managing family responsibilities, traditional goal setting can feel selfish. How do you pursue your dreams when your kids need you? How do you focus on your goals when your spouse is struggling? How do you invest in yourself when everyone else needs your energy?

When you're facing financial stress, traditional goal setting can feel privileged. It's easy to "follow your passion" when you don't have to choose between paying rent and pursuing your dreams. It's simple to "take risks" when you have a safety net.

The worst part? When traditional goal setting doesn't work for you, it makes *you* feel like the problem. Like you're not disciplined enough, motivated enough, or deserving enough. Like success is for other people who have their lives together in ways you don't.

But you're not the problem. The system is.

That's why we need a different approach. One that meets you where you are, honors your reality, and makes room for the full spectrum of human experience.

The SMART Method (Reimagined for Real Life)

Everyone knows that standard SMART goal framework:

- Specific
- Measurable
- Achievable
- Relevant
- Time-bound

You can Google a template, fill in the blanks, and voilà, you have a technically perfect pretty goal. But technically perfect and actually helpful are two different things. Those traditional SMART goals can feel mechanical, soulless, like they were created by someone who's never had to find motivation while drowning in emails, managing a household, or fighting their own mind.

Life is chaotic. You have bad days. You get overwhelmed. You face unexpected challenges. And sometimes, you just need to survive, not thrive.

So, let's reimagine SMART goals for actual humans living actual lives:

S - Soulful (Not Just Specific)

Yes, your goal should be clear, but more importantly, it should matter to you. Not to your boss, your parents, your friends, or the wellness influencer with perfect lighting and zero real problems.

Does this goal light a spark your soul? Does it align with values and what actually matters? If it doesn't connect to something deeper, it's going to fizzle the moment life gets hard.

Your goals should be extensions of who you are, not costumes you're trying to wear. They should feel like coming home, not performing for an audience.

M - Manageable (Not Just Measurable)

Sure, track your progress, but be realistic about what you can manage in the life you're living right now. Not future-you with unlimited time and energy. Today-you, who might be running on 30 minutes of sleep, six cups of coffee, and pure determination.

Instead of "Write for 2 hours every day," try "Write for 15 minutes, three times a week." Instead of "Work out 6 days a week," try "Move my body in some way 4 days a week." Instead of "Read 50 books this year," try "Read 10 pages a day."

Make your goals so manageable that you can't fail. You can always do more, but you need to start with something you can sustain.

A - Adaptable (Not Just Achievable)

Life happens. Kids get sick. Jobs get stressful. Mental health fluctuates. Family drama erupts. Your goals need to be flexible enough to bend without breaking.

Build adaptation into your goals from the beginning. Have Plan A, Plan B, and Plan C, D, E, F, and so on. Know what the bare minimum looks like so you can maintain momentum even on your worst days.

If your plan can't survive a bad week, it's not a plan, it's a wish.

R - Rooted (Not Just Relevant)

Your goals should be deeply rooted in your why. Not what others expect, not what looks good on social media, not what you think you "should" want.

When the going gets tough (and it will), you need to know why you're doing this. You need to be connected to something deeper than external validation, FOMO, or comparison.

Your why should be strong enough to pull you forward when motivation fails, specific enough to guide your decisions, and personal enough to sustain you through the inevitable challenges.

T - Time-Kind (Not Just Time-Bound)

Yes, give yourself a timeline, but make it one that includes room to breathe, rest, and be human. Grace over grind. Progress over pressure. Instead of arbitrary deadlines that add stress, create timelines that motivate without overwhelming. Build in buffer time for life's interruptions. Allow for rest, reflection, and course correction.

You're not racing against anyone else's clock. You're building a life that works for you.

Tools for Tracking Progress (Without Losing Your Mind)

Tracking progress doesn't require color-coded spreadsheets or complicated systems. It requires honest reflection and gentle accountability.

The Progress Journal

Keep it simple. Use a notebook, your phone, or even sticky notes. Write down what worked, what didn't, and how you want to shift fire. No judgment, just observation.

Ask yourself:

- What am I learning about myself?
- What's working better than expected?
- What needs to change?
- How do I want to move forward?

Habit Stacking

Instead of adding entirely new habits, attach new behaviors to things you already do. If you want to meditate, do it right after you brush your teeth. If you want to write, do it while you have your morning coffee. This makes new habits feel less overwhelming and more sustainable.

The Weekly Check-In

To start, set aside 20 minutes every week to check in with your goals like you would with a friend. Ask:

- Am I still excited about this?
- What's going well?
- What feels hard?
- What do I need to adjust?

This isn't about judging your progress. It's about staying connected to your goals and making sure they still serve you.

Celebration Practices

Create specific ways to celebrate your wins, especially the small ones. Finished a chapter? Take a bath. Completed a workout? Dance to your favorite song. Made a difficult phone call? Treat yourself to good coffee.

Celebration reinforces progress and reminds your brain that growth feels good.

The Two-Minute Rule

If a task takes less than two minutes, do it now. If it takes longer, break it down into two-minute pieces. This could help prevent overwhelm and build momentum.

Progress Photos (But Not What You Think)

Take photos of your workspace, your journal, your art, your garden, whatever represents your progress. Visual evidence of growth is powerful, especially on days when you feel stuck.

Reality Check: Don't Go Too Easy on Yourself

Here's some truth wrapped in love: self-compassion doesn't mean self-indulgence. Grace doesn't mean giving up. Being kind to yourself doesn't mean avoiding all discomfort.

Sometimes the most loving thing you can do for yourself is to be honest about where you're holding back, making excuses, or avoiding the work that matters.

Ask yourself:

- Where am I being too comfortable?

- What am I avoiding out of fear rather than genuine overwhelm?
- How am I standing in my own way?
- What would love look like in this situation?

The goal isn't to be harsh with yourself, it's to be honest. There's a difference between the voice of your inner critic (Chapter 2) and the voice of your inner wisdom, which lovingly pushes you toward growth.

Your inner critic:

"You're lazy and you'll never succeed."

Your inner wisdom:

"You're capable of more than you're giving yourself credit for."

Your inner critic:

"You're behind and you're failing."

Your inner wisdom:

"You're exactly where you need to be, and it's time to take the next step."

Learn to distinguish between these voices. One tears you down, the other builds you up while challenging you to grow.

Why This Book Exists: A Personal Story

This book has been living in my heart for years, waiting for the right moment to come alive. Everyone says, "Know your audience before you write." But what if the author is the audience? What if the person you most want to help is yourself? So, I began writing this book as a message to that someone, who turned out to be me.

That's exactly how this started. I told myself, "If someone came to me feeling overwhelmed by a big dream, something that feels impossible, I'd tell them, "You are capable of doing this." When I was young, I shared my dreams with my mama. I also shared the fears. I was bullied, by kids and adults, and just didn't feel like I would ever be someone important. She advocated for me and supported my dreams. "You can get there from here, Punkin', but you have to make sure you do things that will help you."

To start this book, I started with a traditional SMART goal: **Write and complete a 20-chapter self-help book within 6 months by dedicating 1 hour a day, five days a week.**

- **S** — Specific: Write a self-help book consisting of 20 chapters
- **M** — Measurable: Track progress by daily writing sessions of 1 hour, five days a week
- **A** — Achievable: Commit to manageable daily writing that fits into my current schedule
- **R** — Relevant: This goal aligns with my purpose to share helpful guidance with others
- **T** — Time-bound: Complete the book within 6 months

Perfect, right? Textbook goal setting.

And then life happened.

Depression showed up like an uninvited guest and decided to stay. PTSD tied my hands and clouded my thoughts. I was juggling motherhood, marriage, job searching, mental illness diagnoses, and just trying to be present for my family. I'm still a full-time student and PhD candidate, which means my days are already full before I even think about personal projects.

Suddenly, that neat, tidy plan felt like a straitjacket. I couldn't write for an hour a day. Some days, I couldn't write at all. Some days, I was proud of myself for just getting dressed and showing up for my family.

I expected the journey from wanting to write this book to holding it in my hands to be straightforward. But it wasn't. And scrolling through social media, seeing people who seemed to write books overnight, made me question everything. Maybe this wasn't my calling after all. Maybe I wasn't disciplined enough, smart enough, or deserving enough.

I prayed for guidance, for clarity, and for patience. And God answered—not with a dramatic revelation, but through tiny, quiet nudges. Little pieces of the book came to me in unexpected moments. While washing dishes. During my commute. In the middle of conversations with friends. I wrote them down, stored them away, and kept moving forward, one small step at a time.

This experience taught me something crucial about timelines: there is no universal clock for success. Your journey will not look like anyone else's, and that's not just okay, it's perfect. Progress is personal, and sometimes slow progress is the most sustainable kind.

Remember the example of eating an elephant? That's the huge, intimidating goal that seems impossible to tackle. It's overwhelming to stare at the whole thing at once. But you don't have to swallow the elephant in one bite. You just need to take it one small, manageable bite at a time.

The book you're reading right now is proof of that principle. It wasn't written in neat, consecutive sessions. It was written in fragments, in stolen moments, in the spaces between life's demands. It was written during good days and bad days, motivated days and exhausted days, confident days, and doubt-filled days.

And that's exactly why it needed to be written this way. Because this is how real-life works. This is how real people with challenges make real progress toward their dreams.

The Power of Imperfect Progress

Understand that imperfect progress is still progress. Messy movement is still movement. Slow growth is still growth.

You don't have to be perfect to make progress. You don't have to have your life together to work toward your goals. You don't have to wait until you're "ready" because you'll never feel completely ready. You just have to start where you are, with what you have, in the circumstances you're living in right now.

Your goals don't need to be impressive to anyone else. They just need to be meaningful to you. They don't need to fit anyone else's timeline. They just need to fit your life. They don't need to be perfect. They just need to be yours.

The world needs what you have to offer, and it needs it exactly as it comes through you. With all your limitations, challenges, and imperfections. Your unique perspective, shaped by your unique struggles, is exactly what makes your contribution valuable.

So, stop waiting for the perfect moment, the perfect plan, or the perfect version of yourself. Start now, with what you have, where you are. Take one small step, then another, then another. Your dreams are worth pursuing, even imperfectly. Your goals are worth working toward, even slowly. Your progress is worth celebrating, even when it doesn't look like anyone else's.

Creating Your Own Goal-Setting Framework

Based on everything we've discussed, here're nine steps on how to create a goal-setting framework that actually works for your real life.

Step 1: Start with Your Why

Before you set any goals, get clear on why they matter to you. Not why they should matter, not why they matter to others, but why they matter to you specifically. Write it down and make it plain. Habakkuk 2:2. Make it personal. Make it emotional. This is why it will sustain you when motivation fails.

Step 2: Assess Your Reality

Be honest about your current circumstances. What are you dealing with right now? What are your energy levels like? What other commitments do you have? What support do you have available? This isn't about making excuses, but about making realistic plans.

Step 3: Choose One Primary Goal

Focus on one main goal at a time. You can have other smaller goals but choose one that gets most of your attention and energy. Multi-tasking goals is like multi-tasking anything else. It usually means doing several things poorly instead of one thing well.

Step 4: Break It Down

Take your big goal and break it into smaller, manageable pieces. What are the major milestones? What are the weekly actions? What are the daily habits? Make each step so small that you can't fail.

Step 5: Plan for Obstacles

What could go wrong? What usually derails you? What challenges are you likely to face? Plan for these obstacles in advance. Have backup plans, alternative approaches, and minimum viable options.

Step 6: Build in Flexibility

Your plan should be a guide, not a prison. Build in room for life's inevitable interruptions, bad days, and changing circumstances.

Step 7: Create Accountability

Find someone who can support you without judging you. Someone who will celebrate your wins and encourage you through challenges. This could be a friend, family member, coach, or online community. The key is finding people who understand that progress isn't always linear.

Step 8: Schedule Regular Check-Ins

Set aside time regularly to assess your progress and adjust your approach. This keeps you connected to your goals without becoming obsessed with them. Start with 20 minutes a week and adjust when needed.

Step 9: Celebrate Everything

Celebrate small wins, progress, effort, and even beautiful failures. Celebration reinforces positive behaviors and reminds you that the journey matters as much as the destination.

Permission to Proceed Imperfectly

You have permission to set goals that fit your life instead of forcing your life to fit impossible standards. You have permission to move at your own pace, celebrate small wins, and change course when needed. You have permission to be human while pursuing your dreams.

Your goals don't have to be perfect to be powerful. Your progress doesn't have to be consistent to be meaningful. Your journey doesn't have to be smooth to be successful.

What matters is that you keep moving forward, one imperfect step at a time. Don't give up on yourself, even when the path gets hard. Honor your dreams enough to pursue them, even when the pursuit looks different than you imagined. The world needs your unique contribution, and it needs it exactly as it comes through you.

So set those goals. Make those plans. Take those steps. But do it all with grace, flexibility, and plenty of room for the messiness of real life. You can get there from here. You don't have to have it all figured out. You just have to keep going.

One bite at a time.

CHAPTER 5: THE POWER OF THE PIVOT

"PIVOT!" — Ross Geller, carrying a couch and all of us trying to continue.

If you didn't hear the frustrated, close-to-tears voice of Ross Geller when you read "PIVOT!" then we are different kinds of people. Go look it up on YouTube before reading this chapter. Trust me, you'll need the context.

Sometimes growth isn't a steady climb up a mountain. Sometimes it's Ross from "Friends" yelling "PIVOT!" while stuck in a stairwell with a couch that clearly isn't going anywhere, no matter how much you want it to.

We've all been there, haven't we? Maybe not literally wedged in a stairwell, but emotionally? Professionally? Spiritually? Absolutely. We make plans, set goals, create vision boards and five-year trajectories. We invest our hearts, our time, our identity into a path that feels right, feels certain, feels like home.

And then life, in its infinite creativity, shows up with a plot twist: job loss, rejection, illness, heartbreak, or simply the realization that the dream you've been chasing no longer fits the person you've become.

Suddenly, we're trying to wedge the oversized couch of our carefully planned life into a space it no longer fits. And we yell "PIVOT!" at others, sometimes at ourselves, often at the universe.

But here's what I've learned: the power of the pivot isn't about giving up. It's about realigning. It's about recognizing when the path you're on no longer matches the person you're becoming and having the courage to change direction without shame.

You may not be carrying a couch, but maybe you're dragging old goals, outdated roles, or expectations that no longer serve you. This isn't a chapter about quitting. It's a chapter about choosing to honor your growth, to exit with intention, and to make space for what's next. Because sometimes, the most transformational decision isn't pushing forward. It's pausing. Turning. Recalculating. Pivoting.

Why We Resist the Pivot

Let's be honest about why pivoting feels so terrifying. It's not just about changing direction. It's about admitting that the direction you were so sure about might not be the right one anymore. It's about facing the fear that you've "wasted" time, energy, or resources on something that didn't work out.

Resistance to change is just our ego trying to protect us from the discomfort of uncertainty. Our minds prefer the familiar, even when the familiar is no longer serving us. We'd rather stay stuck in a situation we know than risk the unknown, even when the unknown might be exactly where we need to be.

We resist the pivot because:

We're afraid of what others will think. "But you were so passionate about this!" "I thought you were committed!" "You're just giving up!" The fear of judgment can keep us trapped in situations that no longer fit.

We've invested too much to quit now. This is the sunk cost fallacy in action. Just because you've already invested time, money, or energy into something doesn't mean you have to keep investing. Sometimes the most expensive thing you can do is continue paying for something that isn't working.

We don't know what comes next. The devil we know feels safer than the angel we don't. But uncertainty isn't the enemy, it's the space where possibility lives.

We think it means we failed. But pivoting isn't failure. It's growth. It's the recognition that you've outgrown your current situation and are ready for something that better aligns with who you're becoming.

The Art of the Strategic Pivot

Real pivots aren't about panic, they're about power. They're about pausing, breathing, and asking, "Is there another way to do this?" They're about realizing that maybe the couch doesn't belong upstairs anymore, or maybe it's time for a new couch entirely.

Here's how to pivot with intention rather than desperation:

1. Pause and Assess

Before you make any major changes, take time to understand what's really happening. Are you hitting a temporary obstacle, or are you fundamentally misaligned with your path?

Ask yourself:

- What specifically isn't working?
- Is this a problem I can solve, or a signal I need to heed?
- Am I fighting for this because I still want it, or because I've already invested so much?
- What would I do if I were starting fresh today?

2. Separate Your Identity from Your Path

You are not your job, your major, your business, or your plan. You are a complex, evolving human being who is allowed to change course when your path no longer serves your growth.

Your worth isn't tied to your ability to stick to a plan that no longer works. Your value doesn't decrease because you choose to pivot. In fact, your willingness to adapt and grow is often what makes you most valuable.

3. Look for Transferable Skills

Very rarely is a pivot a complete starting over. Most of the time, you're taking valuable skills, experience, and knowledge from one area and applying them in a new context.

What have you learned? What strengths have you developed? What insights have you gained? These aren't lost when you pivot. They're the foundation for what comes next.

4. Reframe the Narrative

Stop telling yourself (and others) that you "failed" or "gave up." Start telling the story of growth, adaptation, and courageous course correction.

Instead of: "I couldn't make it work."

Try: "I learned what I needed to learn and I'm ready for the next chapter."

Instead of: "I wasted all that time."

Try: "That experience prepared me for something better."

Your story isn't about failure, it's about evolution.

When Life Forces Your Hand: Navigating Unwanted Pivots

Sometimes we choose to pivot. Sometimes the pivot chooses us. Job loss, illness, relationship changes, economic shifts—life has a way of making decisions for us that we never would have made for ourselves.

These forced pivots can feel especially devastating because they strip away our sense of control. But they can also be the most transformative, pushing us toward opportunities and growth we never would have pursued otherwise.

When life forces a pivot:

Allow yourself to grieve. You're losing something that matters to you, whether that be a job, a relationship, a dream, an identity. That loss is real, and it deserves to be acknowledged. Give yourself permission to feel sad, angry, or disappointed.

Resist the urge to rush into the next thing. In the discomfort of uncertainty, we often grab the first available option just to feel stable again. But this transition period, as uncomfortable as it is, is valuable. It's where you can reconnect with what you actually want, not just what feels safe.

Look for the gifts in disruption. What opportunities might this change create? What doors might it open? What have you been wanting to try but never had the courage or catalyst to pursue?

Trust the process. Sometimes what feels like the worst thing that could happen is actually the best thing that could happen. The job loss that leads to entrepreneurship. The breakup that leads to self-discovery. The illness that leads to reprioritizing what matters.

My Military Pivot: When the Plan Breaks but the Purpose Remains

Let me tell you about a pivot I never wanted to make but desperately needed to embrace.

I spent nearly ten years in the United States Air Force. Those weren't just years of service, they were years of identity formation, purpose, and belonging. Once I let go of the high school dream of being a stage manager on Broadway, I didn't see the military as a steppingstone or temporary assignment. It became my forever plan, my blueprint for adulthood, my way of being in the world.

I was going to retire after twenty years. I knew I'd make it to E-9. I dreamed of wearing the diamond as a First Sergeant, not for the title or power, but for the privilege of shaping the next generation of Airmen. It was clear. It was certain. It was mine.
Until it wasn't.

Medical complications started to surface. At first, I tried to ignore them, push through, carry the weight silently. I didn't want to be seen as weak or incapable. As a Black woman in Security Forces, a male-dominated career field, I felt the pressure to be twice as strong, twice as tough, twice as resilient.

I told myself, "Just keep going. You'll be fine." The good old southern method. Drink some water and lay down somewhere. But pain doesn't listen to rank, and eventually, I couldn't ignore it anymore.

I had to go to the doctor. I had to be honest about what was happening in my body.

That honesty, while necessary, set everything in motion.

The doctors told me I could no longer remain in the Security Forces career field. I would continue to get hurt if I kept training the way I had been. In a matter of months, the career I had built my life around began to unravel in slow, painful pieces. Law enforcement was in my blood. My daddy was a cop for 30 years, and my uncle was a cop for about the same amount of time. I couldn't fail. I wanted to prove to them that I could do it and make it to retirement like they did.

I tried desperately to hold the frayed ends together. I talked to doctors, filed paperwork. I explored every option, every loophole, every possibility. I wasn't ready to give up. Then someone gave me a sliver of hope: "Your commander can recommend a retrain. If she supports it, you might have a chance."

I didn't waste a second. I went to her office. She wasn't even my permanent commander, just filling in from her Group Deputy Commander position. I explained my situation, laid everything on the table, and asked for her recommendation to stay in the career field I loved. I wasn't asking to be babied or looking for special treatment. I knew I would have to work a little harder to maintain, but Lord, I was willing. I just wanted a chance to stay with my military family. I wanted to finish what I started.

She said no.

She told me I was a liability to the career field. That I couldn't deploy, couldn't carry, couldn't PT. Couldn't be used in Security Forces. She said that keeping me in the Air Force would not benefit the Air Force. I asked again, this time not for my old role, just for her recommendation. A signature. A chance. I would have been okay with Finance or Services, anything that would let me stay.
She refused again. Not with cruelty, not with warmth. Just finality.

I don't know if you've ever had to hold back tears while standing in front of someone with group-level power, but it's an experience that humbles you to the core. I kept my military bearing, thanked her for her time, and walked out of that office with a straight spine and a shattered heart.
That's when the real doubt crept in.

Maybe I shouldn't have gone to the doctor. Maybe I should have just sucked it up. Maybe if I had stayed quiet, I'd still be wearing the uniform. I started blaming myself, replaying every choice that led to that moment. I questioned my worth, my identity, my future.

Even with discharge paperwork being processed, I wouldn't accept it. I called every office I could think of. I emailed everyone who outranked me. I asked questions, pleaded, negotiated. I spent countless hours trying to undo what had already been decided.

I couldn't imagine a life outside the military because I had never planned for one.

I was stuck in that metaphorical stairwell, determined to go up when life was clearly pointing me in a different direction. I was trying to force my couch into a space it no longer fit, and I refused to pivot. But the truth was, the chapter had closed. I was just afraid to let the book end.

June 27, 2017, was my final day in uniform. That's when the fight ended. And the pivot began.

The Pivot I Didn't Want But Desperately Needed

At first, I didn't know how to be a civilian, and they pissed me off. What do you do when everything you built your identity around is suddenly gone? Who are you when you're no longer who you've always been?

I looked around at the pieces of my life and tried to build something new. In October 2017, I opened an in-home daycare. Not only did I open it, but I got the LLC and everything. It wasn't glamorous, and it wasn't what I had envisioned for myself, but it allowed me to contribute. It gave me a reason to get up every day. And quietly, it reminded me that I still had something valuable to offer.

The daycare kept me grounded while my husband continued to serve. It was a bridge between who I had been and who I was becoming. When my husband separated from the military in 2022, our life shifted again. This time, I was ready for the pivot.

I leaned into something I had always loved. Education. I enrolled in a PhD program focused on leadership in higher education. I took everything I had learned in the military, discipline, resilience, mentoring, purpose, and redirected it toward a new mission. I applied for a high school teaching position. And I got it.

Now, I stand in front of classrooms instead of formations. I guide students instead of Airmen. I use my voice, experience, and heart to reach young people who are still figuring out who they want to be. I influence more lives now than I ever imagined I would. Not because I climbed the ranks in uniform, but because I was willing to shift to a new kind of service.

I didn't become a First Sergeant. But I did become a teacher. A mentor. A leader.

And I am fulfilled in ways I never expected.

God, the Author of Pivots

When I think back to those days of fighting so hard to stay in the military, I understand now that I wasn't wrong for trying. I was grieving. I was mourning the loss of a dream, a community, an identity. I was processing the end of one chapter and the terrifying beginning of another. I had told God my plan, laid it out neatly in my prayers, and told Him exactly how it would all go.

He had other ideas.

Not because He was being cruel or because He wanted to see me struggle. But because He already knew that the plan I clung to so tightly was only one chapter in the story He had written for me. He knew that where I was trying to stay was not where I was supposed to be anymore.

Years later, I can say with complete honesty that I am more joyful, impactful, and aligned with my purpose than I ever imagined possible. I am doing exactly what I was meant to do just not in the way

I thought I would do it. I had to release the plan to receive the purpose. And that only happened when I embraced the pivot.

The military gave me discipline, resilience, and leadership skills. But teaching gave me joy, creativity, and the daily opportunity to shape young minds. I needed both experiences to become who I am today. Sometimes God closes doors not to punish us, but to redirect us toward something better. Sometimes the pivot we resist is the pivot that saves us.

How to Pivot with Grace and Wisdom

Based on my experience and the experiences of others who have navigated major life changes, here're seven ways to pivot with intention:

1. Honor What Was

Before you can move forward, you need to acknowledge what you're leaving behind. This isn't about dwelling in the past. It's about recognizing the value of your previous experiences and carrying the lessons forward.

What skills did you develop? What relationships did you build? What insights did you gain? These aren't lost when you pivot. They're the foundation for what comes next.

2. Get Clear on Your Non-Negotiables

What values, principles, or needs must be present in whatever you do next? These non-negotiables will guide your pivot and help ensure that your new direction aligns with who you are at your core.

For me, my non-negotiables were serving others, using my leadership skills, and having a positive impact. Teaching met all of these, even though it looked completely different from my military service.

3. Start Small and Experiment

You don't have to make a complete career change overnight. Start with small experiments, volunteer work, side projects, informational interviews. Test the waters before diving in completely. After I medically retired from the military in Alaska, I worked at my daycare, moved to Illinois, reopened my daycare, worked at Domino's, moved back to Las Vegas, NV, and was a floater, assistant teacher, then assistant director at a daycare, worked in the medical field as a durable medical equipment specialist, volunteered, then became a teacher.

These experiences reduce risk and give you real data about what you enjoy and what you don't, rather than just relying on assumptions.

4. Build Bridges, Don't Burn Them

Maintain relationships and connections from your previous path. You never know when those relationships might be valuable in your new direction. Plus, burning bridges just creates unnecessary drama and limits your options.

5. Invest in New Skills

What do you need to learn or develop to succeed in your new direction? This might mean formal education, certifications, or simply spending time learning from others who are already where you want to be.

6. Find Your Tribe

Surround yourself with people who support your pivot and understand your new direction. This might mean joining new professional organizations, finding mentors, or simply connecting with others who have made similar transitions.

7. Be Patient with the Process

Pivots take time. You're not just changing what you do, you're often changing how you see yourself and how others see you. Be patient with the adjustment period and remember that growth is rarely linear.

The Unexpected Gifts of Pivoting

While pivots can be challenging, they often bring unexpected gifts:

Increased self-awareness. Going through a major change forces you to examine what you really want, what you value, and what makes you happy. This knowledge is invaluable for making better decisions in the future.

Resilience and adaptability. Successfully navigating a pivot builds confidence in your ability to handle change. You learn that you're stronger and more flexible than you thought.

New perspectives. Experiencing different industries, roles, or ways of life broadens your worldview and makes you more empathetic and interesting.

Better alignment. Often, pivots lead us to situations that are better aligned with our values, strengths, and life stage than where we were before.

Expanded network. Each pivot introduces you to new people and new communities, expanding your personal and professional network.

Renewed energy. When you're aligned with your purpose and excited about your direction, you often find energy and motivation you didn't know you had.

Recognizing When It's Time to Pivot

How do you know when it's time to make a change? Here are some signs:

- You feel consistently drained or unfulfilled
- Your values and your daily actions are misaligned
- You find yourself envying others in different situations
- You're going through the motions but not feeling engaged
- You keep having the same problems over and over
- You feel like you've outgrown your current situation
- Your life circumstances have changed significantly
- You have a persistent feeling that there's something else you're supposed to be doing

Trust your intuition. That nagging feeling that something needs to change is usually worth exploring.

Embracing the Plot Twist

Life is not a straight line from Point A to Point B. It's a series of pivots, turns, and course corrections. The sooner you embrace this reality, the less resistance you'll feel when change comes knocking.

Your pivot doesn't have to be perfect. It doesn't have to make sense to everyone else. It doesn't have to be permanent. It just has to be yours.

So, if you find yourself in that metaphorical stairwell—sweating, struggling, stuck—remember that it's okay to let go. It's okay to cry. It's okay to fight for a while. But eventually, you have to ask the harder question: What's waiting for me if I stop pushing and start listening?

The couch might not fit up the stairs. But maybe it belongs in a completely different room. Maybe it's time for a new couch entirely. Maybe the stairwell was never your destination, maybe it was just a pause between where you were and where you need to be.

Your story isn't about the plans that didn't work out. It's about the person you became because you were brave enough to change course when change was needed.

Pivot with grace. Pivot with purpose. Pivot with the understanding that sometimes the best thing you can do is stop trying to force something that was never meant to be and start embracing something that was always meant for you.

The pivot isn't the end of your story. It's the plot twist that makes your story worth telling.

God is good. The pivot is proof.

CHAPTER 6: GET OUT OF YOUR FEELINGS (SOMETIMES)

Let me start by saying this: feelings are not the enemy. They're data. They're clues. They're reminders that we're alive, breathing, and paying attention to our lives. Your emotions serve a purpose, they alert you to danger, help you connect with others, and add color to your experiences.

But, as I have learned the hard way, your feelings are not always right, and they're certainly not always helpful when it's time to get stuff done.

Some days, you'll feel like the main character in your own motivational documentary. Your playlist is perfect, your coffee tastes like liquid ambition, and you're ready to conquer the world. You feel unstoppable, focused, and aligned with your purpose.

But other days? Other days you're the human equivalent of unfolded laundry. You're scrolling social media while your goals sit in the corner collecting dust, telling yourself that tomorrow will definitely be different. You're overwhelmed by a simple to-do list, paralyzed by perfectionism, or plain tired of trying.

We've all been there. This chapter isn't here to shame you for having feelings or to preach the gospel of toxic hustle culture. This isn't about grinding harder or pretending you're a robot who doesn't need rest, comfort, or human connection.

This is a loving but honest conversation about what happens when our emotions become barriers to our goals instead of guides toward our growth.

Let's talk about it.

When Your Feelings Take the Wheel

Imagine for a moment that your feelings are driving the car of your life. Where exactly are they taking you? Are they cruising calmly toward your goals with the windows down and good music playing? Or are they swerving wildly every time something stressful appears on the horizon?

Maybe your fear of failure is white knuckling the steering wheel, slamming on the brakes every time you get close to a breakthrough. Perhaps doubt is riding shotgun with a GPS that's been flipped upside down, shouting "Turn around! We're lost!" even though you're just two miles from your destination.

Maybe anxiety is frantically switching radio stations so fast you can't focus on anything, while procrastination has fallen asleep in the backseat with its feet up. And confidence? Poor confidence is locked in the trunk, pounding on the walls and yelling, "Hey! Remember me? I live here too!" Meanwhile, the twins motivation and discipline called in sick. Again.

When feelings are in the driver's seat, your internal GPS becomes completely unreliable. Every small obstacle feels like a dead end. Every bump in the road feels like a sign from the universe to turn back. You might find yourself parked in the driveway of indecision for days, or worse, doing donuts in the parking lot of "almost started but didn't quite follow through."

The problem isn't that your feelings are terrible drivers, they're just not equipped for the job. Emotions are instinctual, reactive, and immediate. They respond to what's happening right now, not what needs to happen for your future. They're designed to keep you safe in the moment, not navigate you toward long-term success.

Feelings don't plan. They don't strategize. They don't choose the destination based on what's best for your growth. That's your job.

Let's be radical for a moment. What if you let your feelings ride shotgun instead of handing them the keys? What if you acknowledged their presence, heard them out, validated their concerns, but still said, "Thanks for your input, but we're moving forward anyway."

There's a reason pilots are trained to fly through turbulence, not avoid it entirely. Sometimes you have to feel the fear, sadness, anger, overwhelm and still choose the route that leads to your purpose. Your feelings get to come along for the ride. They do not get to drive.

The Difference Between Emotions and Discipline

Here's what I've learned about emotions: they're powerful, but they're also unreliable narrators. They tell compelling stories that feel absolutely true in the moment, but those stories aren't always accurate or helpful.

Emotions are like weather. They change constantly, sometimes without warning, and they're largely outside of your control. You can't decide to stop feeling anxious any more than you can decide to stop a thunderstorm. But you can decide how to respond to both.

If sadness makes all your decisions, you'll never get up. If fear runs the show, you'll never try. If insecurity calls the shots, you'll always shrink. If procrastination takes the wheel, you'll keep spinning in circles.

Discipline, on the other hand, is steady. It's a quiet commitment to act in alignment with your values and goals, regardless of how you feel in the moment. Where emotions can push you to start something new in a burst of inspiration, discipline is what helps you finish when that initial spark inevitably fades.

Discipline doesn't require emotional permission. It just needs a decision.

Think about it: you brush your teeth even when you don't feel like it. You go to work even when you'd rather stay in bed. You pay your bills even when you'd rather spend that money on something fun. These actions aren't driven by emotion. They're driven by discipline and the understanding that some things need to happen regardless of how you feel about them.

Your goals deserve the same treatment.

Funk is Real (And So Is Your Power to Move Through It)

Before I go any further, let me be crystal clear: I'm not talking about ignoring mental illness, clinical depression, or genuine psychological distress. I live with mental health challenges myself, and I would never minimize that reality or suggest that people should just "think positive" their way out of serious conditions.

I'm talking about the everyday emotional fog that can descend on any of us. The days when everything feels harder than it should, when motivation is nowhere to be found, and when your thoughts feel like quicksand.

The funk is real. It's not imaginary, it's not weakness, and it's definitely not just laziness. You can wake up feeling off for no identifiable reason. You might find yourself tearing up at commercials, irritated by sounds you usually don't notice, or completely paralyzed by a simple to-do list. You sit on the edge of your bed staring at a pile of laundry like it personally betrayed you.

I get it. I've been there more times than I can count.

But here's what I've learned after crawling through that fog repeatedly. You don't think your way out of it. You move your way out. One small, defiant act at a time. One dish washed. One step outside. One text returned. One page read. One paragraph written.

That first movement might feel completely mechanical, like you're going through the motions without any real feeling behind it. And that's okay. That mechanical action interrupts the spiral. It breaks the pattern of staying stuck in your feelings.

Action doesn't just create external results. It creates internal rhythm. And rhythm leads to momentum. And momentum leads to more action. That's where discipline lives. Not in grand, heroic gestures, but in the tiniest moments of resistance against the voice that says, "I can't."

You don't need to feel better to start. You just need to start. That could be slowly, gently, imperfectly. The feelings may not disappear overnight, but when you move, even through the heaviness, you remind yourself of something powerful. You're still here. You're still capable. And you're not done yet.

Building Systems for Your Lowest Days

The key to getting out of your feelings isn't willpower but systems. Systems are the structures and habits you create to keep moving forward when you don't feel like moving at all.

Most people believe motivation and discipline are synonymous, but they are not. Motivation is like a spark. It's bright and powerful but often fleeting. It comes and goes with your mood, your environment, your latest Instagram inspiration, or how many people liked your social media post. Discipline, on the other hand, is built into your life. It's the muscle you develop over time through consistent practice.

Discipline doesn't rely on feeling "up for it" because it's woven into your routine and mindset. It's automatic, like breathing.

That's where systems come in. They support your future self when your present self is an emotional puddle on the floor. They remove the need for constant decision-making and make progress almost automatic.

1. Create One Non-Negotiable Habit

Pick one thing. One tiny action. Something that takes five minutes or less. Make it small.

Write one sentence. Walk to the mailbox. Read one page. Send one email. Do five push-ups. Meditate for two minutes.

The goal isn't to accomplish something massive, it's to prove to yourself that you can still act even when you don't feel like it. That proof becomes the foundation for bigger actions later.

2. Use the Two-Minute Rule

If something takes less than two minutes, do it immediately. If it takes longer, break it down into two-minute chunks and do one chunk.

This prevents overwhelm and builds momentum. Instead of "write my book," it becomes "write one paragraph." Instead of "clean the house," it becomes "wash five dishes."

Small actions compound into big results, but only if you start with actions that feel manageable.

3. Prepare for Your Emotional Weather

Just like you check the weather forecast to decide what to wear, you can prepare for your emotional weather by having backup plans.

What will you do on days when anxiety is high? What's your plan for when depression hits? How will you handle overwhelm? Having predetermined responses removes the burden of decision-making when you're already struggling.

4. Track Actions, Not Feelings

Don't measure your success by how you felt while doing something but measure it by whether you did it. Some of your best work will come from your hard days, when you showed up despite feeling terrible.

Keep a simple record. "Today I did X, even though I felt Y." This creates evidence that you're capable of action regardless of your emotional state.

5. Build Your Accountability Network

Shame keeps us trapped in our feelings. Accountability pulls us out. Tell someone about your goals, not just the pretty, inspiring parts, but the real, messy, daily grind parts.

Find people who can remind you of who you are when you forget. People who will say, "I know you don't feel like it, but let's do it anyway" instead of "Oh, you poor thing, just wait until you feel better."

6. Write Down Your Why

Not just floating around in your head where it can get muddled by emotions. Write it down. Make it concrete. Frame it. Make it your phone background. Print it out and stick it on your bathroom mirror.

When your emotions scream, "I can't," your written why can whisper back, "But this is why you must."

What About Real Mental Health Struggles?

I need to pause here and make something absolutely clear: if your feelings are more than just temporary low motivation—if you're dealing with clinical depression, anxiety disorders, trauma, or other mental health conditions—please don't just "push through." That's not strength. That's suffering in silence.

Ask for help. Talk to someone qualified. Therapy, medication, rest, professional support, these are healing tools, not signs of weakness. You're not lazy. You're not broken. You're a human being who deserves care and treatment.

Getting out of your feelings sometimes doesn't mean ignoring them always. It means learning to distinguish between feelings that provide useful information and feelings that are keeping you stuck.

If you're in crisis, get help immediately. If you're dealing with ongoing mental health challenges, work with professionals to develop strategies that work for your specific situation.

What I'm talking about in this chapter is the daily dance between feeling and action that we all navigate, whether we have mental health diagnoses or not.

No Excuses, Only Ownership: My Story

Let me get personal again for a moment, because I think it's important for you to understand where this chapter comes from.

Some people might look at my medical chart and think they have me figured out. PTSD. Major Depressive Disorder. Bipolar II. Adjustment Disorder. ADHD. Autism Spectrum Disorder. Generalized Anxiety Disorder. Panic Disorder. That's quite a list, isn't it? Add to that the constant commentary about my weight from every doctor I see. At 5'10" and 210 pounds, somehow my weight becomes relevant to every single medical appointment, even when I'm there for something completely unrelated. I could walk in with a broken arm, and they'd still point to the scale first.

Yes, I'm prediabetic. Yes, my medication list is long enough to stock a small pharmacy. And no, I don't "suffer from" these conditions. I live with them. There's a difference.

My diagnoses are not the headline of my life. They're footnotes. Information, not identity.

What's true about me doesn't live in the labels on a medical chart. It lives in the life I've built despite and alongside those labels. I am, first and foremost, an undeserving child of God, who received his grace, mercy, and favor every day, fresh like dew in the morning. Proverbs 19:12. I've been married to my high school sweetheart, my first and only boyfriend, for 20 years this September. We've been together for 23 years total on the same date. We've raised two boys, now 16 and 12, who are safe, provided for, and deeply loved. They want for nothing because we made their wellbeing our mission.

We broke generational cycles without a blueprint. Our marriage is one of the longest-standing relationships among our siblings and cousins. We served this country together as proud members of the United States Air Force. We've seen the world, built a home, and loved our families with action, not just words.

We pour into others because of the grace we received from those who came before us. We teach our sons faith, resilience, responsibility, and honor. We're building something that will outlast us.

That is my story. That is who I am.

But I'll be honest, I haven't always claimed this narrative. For years, I coddled myself with phrases like "You're going through so much" and "You're doing the best you can." Sometimes that compassion was necessary and healing. But most of the time, it was just permission to stay stuck. It was a back door out of accountability. I let my very real pain become my excuse for not pursuing my very real dreams.

I used to rehearse all the reasons I couldn't succeed. The depression, anxiety, trauma, weight, medications, side effects, medications for the side effects, bad days, overwhelming days, days I could barely get dressed. I had a whole catalog of perfectly valid reasons why I couldn't be expected to show up fully for my own life.

Everything changed when I stopped lying to myself about what I was capable of.

I had to get brutally honest about how many opportunities I had let slide by because I was too busy surviving on sympathy instead of thriving on strength. I had to confront the uncomfortable truth that while my struggles were real, my excuses had become bigger than my efforts.

The day I started holding myself to a higher standard, not a cruel or unrealistic standard, but a standard that honored my actual capabilities—everything shifted. I stopped collecting evidence of why I couldn't and started building proof that I could.

That's when discipline showed up. Not before. Not when I felt better. Not when life got easier. When I decided to stop using my challenges as permission slips to stay small.

The Power of "Anyway" and "Any Way"

The most powerful word and phrase in my vocabulary has become "anyway" and "any way."

They have two separate meanings:

Anyway means regardless.

Any way means by any means necessary.

I feel anxious...I'm going to make that phone call anyway and any way. I feel overwhelmed...I'm going to write one paragraph anyway and any way. I feel tired...I'm going to take that walk anyway and any way. I feel like giving up...I'm going to try one more time anyway and any way.

"Anyway" and "any way" are the bridge between feeling and action. It acknowledges your emotional reality without being controlled by it. It says, "I see your feelings, but we're moving forward regardless." This isn't about suppressing emotions or pretending they don't matter. It's about refusing to let them make all your decisions for you.

Your feelings are valid. Your struggles are real. Your challenges matter. And you're going to pursue your goals anyway and any way.

Practical Strategies for Emotional Days

Here are some concrete strategies I use when my emotions are trying to run the show:

The Five-Minute Rule

Commit to doing something for just five minutes. Often, starting is the hardest part, and once you begin, momentum carries you forward. If you stop after five minutes, that's fine. You kept your commitment to yourself.

The Bare Minimum List

Create a list of the absolute minimum you need to do to keep your life and goals moving forward. On emotional days, just do the bare minimum. No guilt, no judgment, just the basics.

The Feeling-Action Gap

Put space between feeling something and acting on it. Feel frustrated? Count to ten before deciding whether to quit. Feel overwhelmed? Take three deep breaths before choosing your next action.

The Evidence Collection

When emotions tell you stories about your limitations, collect evidence to the contrary. Keep a list of things you've accomplished during difficult times. Remind yourself of your resilience.

The Future Self Check-In

Ask yourself: "What would my future self thank me for doing right now?" Usually, it's not wallowing in the emotion. It's taking one small step forward.

A Note for the Dreamer Who's Stuck

If you're reading this and feeling like you've lost your fire, this chapter is your match. You're not broken just because your motivation faded. You're not failing because you need to cry before you try again.

Feel the feelings. Then do the thing. Cry, then keep going. Doubt yourself, then take the step anyway any way. Complain a little if you need to, then move forward.

You're allowed to be human. You're allowed to have bad days, emotional reactions, and moments of weakness. But don't forget, you're also powerful. You're also capable. You're also resilient.

You can be both vulnerable and strong. You can acknowledge your struggles and still pursue your dreams. You can honor your emotions without being enslaved by them.

The Truth About Discipline

Here's what discipline is: it's not about becoming emotionless or superhuman. It's about developing the ability to act in alignment with your values and goals even when your emotions are pulling you in a different direction.

Discipline is saying "I'm going to do this" and then doing it, regardless of whether you feel like it in the moment. Discipline is keeping promises to yourself, especially the small ones. Discipline is choosing long-term satisfaction over short-term comfort. Discipline is showing up for your dreams even when your dreams feel impossible. Discipline is not a personality trait you're born with. It's a skill you develop through practice. And like any skill, it gets stronger the more you use it.

You Are Not Your Feelings

Your feelings are part of your human experience, but they are not the totality of who you are. You are not your anxiety. You are not your depression. You are not your overwhelm. You are not your doubt.

Let me hype you up for you. You are the person who experiences these things and chooses how to respond to them. You are the person who can feel afraid and act courageously anyway. You are the person who can feel sad and still show up for your responsibilities. You are the person who can feel overwhelmed and still take one small step forward.

Your feelings are temporary visitors, not permanent residents. They come and go, but your commitment to your goals can remain constant.

So, feel what you need to feel. Honor your emotional reality. Seek support when you need it. Take care of your mental health. Rest when you need to rest.

And then, get out of your feelings and into your purpose.

Your dreams are waiting for you. They don't care how you feel today. They just care that you show up.

So, show up. Anyway any way.

CHAPTER 7: SUPPORT IS NICE, BUT YOU'RE THE STAR

Support feels good. There's no denying it. Encouragement from friends, family, mentors, or coaches can lift your spirits and propel you forward when times get tough. Having people who believe in you, who see your potential when you can't see it yourself, who cheer you on from the sidelines is valuable. It's beautiful. It's part of what makes us human.

The hard truth is that the real power to create lasting success and fulfillment doesn't live in their hands. It lives in yours.

You are the star of your own story, and no one else can play that lead role for you. No one else can want your dreams more than you do. No one else can do the work that only you can do. And no one else can give you the permission you're waiting for to become who you're meant to be.

This chapter isn't about rejecting help or becoming an island. It's about understanding the difference between support that empowers you and support that makes you dependent. It's about learning to be your own biggest fan, your own best advocate, and your own most reliable source.

Because if you can't believe in yourself when nobody else is watching, all the applause in the world won't be enough to sustain you.

The Applause Trap

Lady Gaga knew what she was talking about when she sang about "living for the applause." That thrill of recognition, the rush of external validation, the intoxicating feeling of being seen and celebrated can become addictive.

We live in a culture that's designed to make us crave applause. Social media platforms are built on likes, shares, and comments. Our education system rewards us with grades and gold stars. Our workplaces use performance reviews and public recognition. From childhood, we're conditioned to look outside ourselves for proof that we're doing well.

And there's nothing inherently wrong with enjoying recognition. The problem comes when your motivation, your sense of worth, or your ability to keep going depends entirely on that external validation.

When you live for the applause, you're essentially putting your power in someone else's hands. You're saying, "I can only feel good about myself if you tell me I should." You're making your emotional well-being dependent on the reactions of people who may be too busy, too distracted, or too caught up in their own lives to notice your efforts.

Reality is the applause isn't guaranteed. Some days, you'll work your hardest and hear nothing in return. You'll pour your heart into something meaningful and receive silence. You'll achieve something significant and watch as the world barely notices.

If your entire sense of purpose and self-worth depends on external validation, those silent moments will devastate you. You'll start questioning your value, your efforts, your dreams. You'll begin to believe that if no one is clapping, maybe what you're doing doesn't matter.

The applause trap is the belief that your worth is determined by how loudly others cheer for you.

Learning to Be Your Own Audience

True fulfillment, the kind that lasts through both celebration and silence, comes from something deeper than external recognition. It comes from the quiet conviction that you are enough, whether anyone else sees it or not. It comes from knowing that your work matters, your growth matters, your efforts matter, regardless of who notices.

This doesn't mean you become indifferent to feedback or recognition. It means you don't need them to know your own value.

When you learn to be your own primary audience, you become unstoppable. No silence can break your spirit because you're not performing for the people in the back row but for the person who matters most. You.

This shift changes everything. Instead of waiting for permission to feel proud of your work, you give yourself that permission. Instead of looking for external validation to know you're on the right track, you develop internal navigation. Instead of measuring your worth by others' reactions, you measure it by your own growth, effort, and alignment with your values.

Building Unshakeable Self-Trust

Self-trust is the foundation of inner strength. It's what allows you to rely on yourself when the world feels unreliable. It's what gives you the confidence to keep going when others doubt you, or worse, when you doubt yourself.

But self-trust isn't something you're born with, it's something you build, one small promise at a time.

Every time you do what you say you're going to do, you make a deposit in your self-trust account. Every time you follow through on a commitment to yourself, no matter how small, you prove to yourself that you're dependable. Every time you honor your word to yourself, you strengthen the relationship you have with the most important person in your life. You.

On the flip side, every time you break a promise to yourself, you withdraw from that account. Every time you talk yourself out of something you said you'd do, every time you make excuses instead of making progress, every time you choose immediate comfort over long-term growth, you chip away at your self-trust.

This is why self-trust feels fragile at first, especially if you've spent years breaking promises to yourself. But it grows stronger with practice. The more you prove to yourself that you can be counted on, the more you'll trust yourself to handle whatever comes your way. Building self-trust starts with small, manageable commitments:

- If you say you'll write for 10 minutes, write for 10 minutes
- If you say you'll go for a walk, go for a walk
- If you say you'll make that phone call, make that phone call
- If you say you'll get up at a certain time, get up at that time

These might seem insignificant, but they're not. Each kept promise is proof that you can rely on yourself. Each follow-through builds evidence that you're someone who does what they say they'll do.

Developing Resilience That Can't Be Shaken

Self-trust naturally leads to resilience, which is the ability to bounce back from difficulties, to face failures without falling apart, and to keep going when the road gets tough.

Resilience isn't about being tough all the time or never feeling hurt by setbacks. It's about knowing that you can handle whatever comes your way because you've handled hard things before. It's about trusting your ability to figure things out, to adapt, to learn, to grow through challenges rather than despite them.

When you have resilience built on self-trust, you stop fearing failure because you know that failure won't break you, it will teach you. You stop needing constant reassurance because you trust your ability to make good decisions and course-correct when needed. You also stop depending on perfect conditions because you know you can make progress in any conditions.

Resilience is like muscle. It gets stronger every time you use it. Every challenge you face and overcome, every setback you bounce back from, every moment you choose to keep going when giving up would be easier build your resilience.

When the Applause Fades: My Wake-Up Call

Let me tell you about the day my husband asked me a question that changed everything.

I was working as a medical care specialist, coordinating the ordering of durable medical equipment (DME) through multiple companies and catalogues, scheduling doctors' appointments at multiple hospitals with numerous physicians, and advocating for individuals who had served in high-risk environments like nuclear energy fields. I had well over 200 clients. Saying as though many of my clients had terminal illnesses from their work, I was on the team of people who would care for them until they died.

It was meaningful work. I felt it was work that mattered and helped people who had sacrificed for our country through military service and with work at test sites.

But I felt invisible.

That day, I was feeling especially low. I had been pouring everything I had, my time, energy, brainpower, and heart, into my job, but I felt like no one noticed. No one had said "thank you" or "good job" or even acknowledged that I was working hard. And even though I knew I was doing important work, something inside me desperately needed someone else to say it.

My husband and I were spending time together, just driving around town, going to different stores, nothing fancy. At some point, I opened up about how discouraged I felt. I told him I was tired and sad because no one was acknowledging my efforts. I needed someone to tell me I was doing a great job, and it wasn't happening.

He listened, like the amazing husband he is, and waited until I was done pouring my heart out before he responded.

Then he asked me a question that hit like a lightning bolt. "Why do you need someone to come tell you that you're doing a good job? Isn't it enough that you know you are?"

I won't lie to you. I was offended. I crossed my arms, looked out the window of the car, and shut down. The audacity! How dare he suggest that I was just chasing applause? How dare he act like needing recognition was some character flaw?

But his question kept echoing in my mind, tapping at something deeper that I didn't want to examine.

By the time we were browsing in Ross (best store ever), those words had burrowed under my irritation and started working on something I'd been avoiding. Why did I need that external validation so badly? When did I start measuring my worth by other people's reactions?

The realization was uncomfortable. I had outsourced my sense of value. If an email came with praise, I felt ten feet tall. If it didn't, I shrank. My emotional thermostat was wired to someone else's applause meter, and I was exhausted from the constant temperature changes.

I'd prided myself on being competent and independent, yet here I was, waiting for a gold star like a kid waving a complete worksheet.

No wonder I felt drained! I was running a marathon while constantly looking around for a cheering section that might never appear.

The Shift: Becoming My Own Biggest Fan

That conversation planted a seed that didn't bloom immediately. I was still feeling some type of way about being called out so bluntly. But it began to shift something in me. I started asking myself different questions. "Can I honor my own hard work?" "Can I look in the mirror and say, *you're doing great*, and believe it even if no one else ever says it?"

I started listing my wins, even when no one else noticed them. Again, I won't lie to you, I initially started doing it because my feelings were still hurting. That week, I helped a client get DME equipment they desperately needed. I successfully staffed a difficult 24-hour care case with a PCA, CNA and an RN. I had convinced a client that he was worth the increase in his care hours and wasn't a burden to anyone. I had secured an earlier medical appointment with a client who was in pain.

Each item initially sounded small when I listed it, but together they formed a chorus I'd been too busy waiting for external applause to hear. My husband confirmed the impact I was making, but more importantly, I started to see it for myself.

This wasn't about becoming arrogant or dismissive of feedback. It was about learning to recognize my own value independent of others' recognition of it.

Strategies for Owning Your Narrative

Taking control of your story means refusing to let other people's reactions (or lack thereof) define your worth. Here are practical ways to build your own internal support system:

1. Keep a Win Journal

Every day, write down at least three things you did well, no matter how small. Made your bed? That's a win. Had a difficult conversation? That's a win. Helped someone? That's a win. This trains your brain to notice your own progress instead of waiting for others to point it out.

2. Celebrate Your Efforts, Not Just Results

Results aren't always within your control, but effort is. Celebrate the fact that you tried, that you showed up, that you gave your best with what you had. This builds resilience because it's not dependent on external outcomes.

3. Develop Your Own Standards of Success

Instead of using other people's definitions of success, create your own. What does a successful day look like to you? What does progress look like in your specific circumstances? When you have your own standards, you don't need others to validate whether you're meeting them.

4. Practice Self-Encouragement

Talk to yourself the way you would talk to a friend you love. When you're struggling, offer yourself compassion. When you succeed, offer yourself congratulations. Become fluent in the language of self-support.

5. Build a Values-Based Identity

Instead of defining yourself by your achievements or others' opinions, define yourself by your values. Are you kind? Hardworking? Honest? Creative? These qualities exist regardless of external recognition.

6. Create Your Own Applause

Literally. When you accomplish something, even something small, clap for yourself. Say "good job" out loud. Take yourself out to celebrate. Don't wait for others to throw you a party. Throw your own.

The Difference Between Support and Dependency

There's a crucial difference between support and dependency:

Support encourages your independence and growth. It celebrates your successes and helps you learn from your failures. It empowers you to trust yourself more, not less.

Dependency makes you reliant on external validation for your sense of worth. It creates anxiety when approval isn't forthcoming and makes you question your value based on others' reactions.

Good support systems, whether they're friends, family, mentors, or communities, should help you develop your own internal strength, not replace it.

When Nobody's Watching

The true test of your internal foundation comes when nobody's watching. Do you still show up when there is no applause or recognition? Do you still do good work? Do you still pursue your goals?

If the answer is yes, you've developed something powerful called intrinsic motivation. You're no longer performing for the crowd; you're living for yourself and your values. This doesn't mean you stop appreciating recognition when it comes. It means you don't need it to keep going.

Building Your Inner Audience

Your inner audience is made up of the values, standards, and dreams that guide you from within. It's the part of you that knows when you've done good work, even if no one else notices. It's the part of you that celebrates growth, effort, and integrity over external rewards.

To build your inner audience:

Clarify your values. What matters most to you? What kind of person do you want to be? Let these values be your guide and your measure of success.

Set personal standards. What does excellence look like to you? What standards do you want to hold yourself to, regardless of what others expect?

Develop internal rewards. Create ways to celebrate and motivate yourself that don't depend on other people. Maybe it's taking a relaxing bath after a hard day or treating yourself to something special after reaching a goal.

Practice self-reflection. Regularly check in with yourself about how you're doing. Are you living up to your own standards? Are you growing? Are you proud of your efforts?

The Ripple Effect of Self-Reliance

When you stop needing constant external validation, something beautiful happens, you become a source of validation for others. When you're secure in your own worth, you can celebrate others without feeling threatened. When you trust your own judgment, you can offer genuine support without needing anything in return.

People are drawn to those who are secure in themselves. Your self-reliance doesn't make you isolated, it actually makes you more attractive as a friend, partner, and colleague because you're not constantly draining energy from others to fill your own emotional tank.

The Truth About Independence

Being the star of your own story doesn't mean you never need help or support. It means you don't make other people responsible for your emotional well-being or sense of worth. You can appreciate encouragement without depending on it. You can enjoy recognition without requiring it. You can accept help without becoming helpless.

True independence isn't about doing everything alone, it's about taking full responsibility for your own life, choices, and emotional state while still being open to connection and support.

Take the Stage

The spotlight of your life is always on, whether anyone else is watching or not. You're performing every day, whether that be for your own values, your own growth, your own purpose.

Stop waiting for permission to feel proud of your work. Stop looking for validation that you're on the right path. Stop needing others to tell you that you matter.

You matter because you exist. Your work matters because you put your heart into it. Your dreams matter because they're yours.

The world may not always applaud, but you don't need it to. You have front-row access to your own story. You know the effort you put in, the obstacles you overcome, the growth you achieve. You know when you're living up to your potential and when you're not.

So today, if you're tired of waiting to be seen, let this be your moment. See yourself. Acknowledge your own efforts. Celebrate your own progress. Give yourself the recognition you've been waiting for others to provide.

Because here's the truth: if you don't believe in your own worth, all the applause in the world won't convince you. But if you do believe in it, deep in your bones, you'll never need to chase external validation again.

You'll be too busy living, creating, growing, and shining from a place of genuine self-worth that can't be dimmed by silence or brightened by applause.

You are the star of your own story. It's time to take the stage and own it. The only standing ovation you really need is the one you give yourself.

CHAPTER 8: WHO SAID THAT? (AND WHY YOU BELIEVED THEM)

We all carry voices in our heads that aren't our own. They whisper limitations, shout impossibilities, and declare verdicts about our futures as if they were facts carved in stone. These voices belong to teachers who labeled us, doctors who delivered diagnoses like death sentences, parents who projected their fears onto our dreams, and strangers who thought they knew us better than we knew ourselves.

But here's the question that will change your life: who said that? And more importantly, why did you believe them?

This chapter is about the lies we've been told about ourselves and the power we've given those lies to shape our reality. It's about recognizing that someone else's opinion, no matter how educated, experienced, or authoritative they seem, is still just an opinion. And opinions, even expert ones, can be wrong.

Very, very wrong.

The Authority Trap

We're taught to trust authority figures from the moment we're born. Teachers, doctors, parents, coaches, bosses. We're conditioned to believe that their words carry more weight than our own inner knowing. And in many cases, this serves us well. We need guidance, wisdom, and expertise from those who've gone before us.

But somewhere along the way, we start treating opinions like facts and possibilities like certainties. We take someone's assessment of our limitations and make it our life sentence. We accept their version of our story and stop writing our own.

The problem isn't that we listen to experts. It's that we sometimes forget they're humans. They have biases, limited perspectives, and incomplete information. They base their assessments on statistics, patterns, and past experiences, but they can't account for the power of human will, divine intervention, or the countless variables that make each person's journey unique.

When someone in authority tells you what you can't do, can't have, or can't become, they're making a prediction based on their limited understanding of your infinite possibilities. They're not prophets. They're people. And people, even well-meaning, highly educated people, can be wrong.

The Birth of Limiting Beliefs

Most of our limiting beliefs were planted when we were too young, too trusting, or too vulnerable to question them. A teacher said you weren't smart enough. A coach said you weren't athletic enough. A parent said you weren't careful enough. A doctor said you weren't healthy enough.

These statements, delivered at crucial moments in our development, burrowed deep into our subconscious, and became the foundation for how we see ourselves and what we believe is possible for our lives.

The tragedy isn't just that we believed in these limitations. It's that we made them true by living within their boundaries. We didn't pursue opportunities because we "weren't smart enough." We didn't try new things because we "weren't athletic enough." We played small because we weren't "enough" of anything.

But those authority figures didn't tell you that their words were assessments of a moment, not prophecies of a lifetime. They were describing what they saw then, not declaring what would always be. They were offering their perspective, not revealing your destiny.

When Doctors Become Fortune Tellers

Let me tell you about the day I learned that medical degrees don't come with crystal balls.

I was fourteen years old when doctors told me I would never have children. Not "it might be difficult" or "you may face challenges." Never. They said it was due to twisted tubes, something wrong with my uterus, the specific details of which I don't even remember. All I knew was that I had been given a medical verdict: a one-in-a-million chance of having children.

I believed them. Why wouldn't I? They were doctors! They had charts, test results, medical degrees hanging on their walls. They spoke with the authority of science and statistics. Who was I, a fourteen-year-old girl, to question their expertise?

That diagnosis followed me for years. It became part of my identity, part of how I saw my future. When I thought about my life, I planned around that limitation. It wasn't just that I couldn't have children, it was that I was someone who couldn't have children. There's a difference. One is about circumstances; the other is about identity.

When I married my husband, we had already agreed that we wanted a family. We talked about adoption, about being a couple who would love children that others couldn't care for. We were at peace with our path, trusting that God would give us the family we were meant to have.

And then, at twenty-two, I got pregnant.

I remember staring at that positive pregnancy test, my hands shaking, tears streaming down my face. The doctors had been wrong. The one-in-a-million chance had happened. The impossible had become possible.

But even then, the voice of that diagnosis whispered in my ear. The doctors had said I would never have children. They hadn't said I would never get pregnant. In my mind, I convinced myself that this was the cruel fulfillment of that prophecy. I would get pregnant, but I wouldn't have children. Something would go wrong.

A Pregnancy Wrapped in Fear

It wasn't an easy pregnancy. I was 340 pounds, 5'10", serving in the United States Air Force as law enforcement. My body was already under stress from the demands of my job, and now it was trying to sustain a life while carrying the weight of that old diagnosis.

I had to collect my urine for protein tests. I had to complete stress tests twice a week. There was low fetal movement, low amniotic fluid, gestational diabetes. Every complication felt like confirmation that the doctors had been right, I would never have children. I was just going to get pregnant and lose this baby I already loved so desperately.

My son's heart rate would drop to terrifyingly low levels during those stress tests. I'd lie there on the table, sensors attached to my belly, listening to that irregular heartbeat and thinking, "This is it. This is how the prophecy comes true."

At 36 weeks, they decided too much was going wrong, and he needed to come out. Four weeks early, by emergency cesarean, he was delivered into a world where his mother was convinced she was living out a medical curse.

The delivery was difficult. I had complications with my blood pressure and other issues that made everything feel more dangerous, more uncertain. But then I heard the most beautiful sound in the world.

He cried. Loud and strong and furious. His cries sounded exactly like he was yelling, "I'm mad!" as if he was offended by being forced out of his warm, comfortable home four weeks ahead of schedule.

Eight pounds, twelve ounces of pure miracle. Healthy, whole, and very much alive. The doctors had been wrong.

The Second Miracle

Five years later, I got pregnant again. This time, I didn't spend the pregnancy waiting for disaster. I had proof that the doctors' verdict wasn't my destiny. I had evidence that their expertise had limitations.

My second son arrived, 39 weeks, planned cesarean, 8lbs 13oz, healthy and perfect, another testament to the fact that medical predictions are not divine decrees. Another reminder that "never" is not a word that applies to God's plans.

As I write this, my 16-year-old is upstairs, probably gaming with his friends. My 12-year-old also upstairs, probably watching tv, bothering his brother, or thinking about the 350,000 Bells he has in Animal Crossing and how he's going to spend them. They are both miracles walking around my house, living proof that someone else's limitations don't have to become your reality.

Two boys who, according to medical expertise, should never have existed. Two sons who are here because we chose to trust God's plan over man's predictions.

The Ripple Effect of Rewritten Stories

When you challenge one limiting belief successfully, it creates a ripple effect. If the doctors were wrong about my ability to have children, what other "expert opinions" about my life might be wrong too? What other "impossibilities" might be possibilities waiting for the right conditions?

This experience taught me to hold expert opinions with an open hand. I still seek medical advice, still value professional expertise, but I no longer treat human assessment as divine revelation. I've learned to ask better questions:

- Is this opinion based on statistics or certainties?
- Are there exceptions to this rule?
- What factors might this expert not be considering?
- How does this align with what I know about myself?
- What would happen if I chose to believe differently?

Unpacking Your Limiting Beliefs

Most of us carry limiting beliefs so deeply embedded in our consciousness that we don't even recognize them as beliefs. We think they're facts. But if you look closely, you can trace almost every limitation you believe about yourself back to a person, a moment, a voice that told you what you couldn't do.

Common Sources of Limiting Beliefs:

> **Teachers**: "You're not college material." "You're not good at math." "You're too quiet to be a leader."

> **Parents**: "Money doesn't grow on trees." "People like us don't do things like that." "Don't get your hopes up."

> **Coaches**: "You're not fast enough." "You don't have the right build for this sport." "Some people are just naturally talented."

> **Doctors**: "You'll never fully recover." "This is just something you'll have to live with." "At your age, you shouldn't expect..."

> **Employers**: "You're not management material." "This industry isn't for people like you." "You should be grateful for what you have."

> **Society**: Messages about age, gender, race, background, education, or appearance that suggest what you can or can't achieve.

Identifying Your Limiting Beliefs:

Pay attention to the thoughts that start with:

- "I could never..."
- "I'm not the type of person who..."
- "People like me don't..."
- "I'm too old/young/inexperienced/whatever to..."
- "That's just not realistic for someone like me..."

Ask yourself: where did this belief come from? Who first told you this wasn't possible? What evidence do you have that it's true?

Techniques for Rewriting Your Narrative

1. Question the Source

When you identify a limiting belief, investigate its origin. Who told you this? What were their qualifications to make this declaration about your life? What might they have been wrong about? Were they speaking from their own fears or limitations?

2. Look for Evidence to the Contrary

For every limiting belief, there are exceptions. If someone told you that people your age don't start new careers, find examples of people who did. If someone said people from your background don't succeed in certain fields, research those who have.

3. Reframe the Story

Instead of "I can't because..." try "I haven't yet because..." The first is a declaration of permanent limitations; the second is a statement of current circumstances that can change.

4. Separate Fact from Opinion

Learn to distinguish between factual statements and subjective assessments. "You failed this test" is fact. "You're not smart enough for this program" is opinion.

5. Create New Evidence

The most powerful way to overcome a limiting belief is to prove it wrong through action. Take small steps toward what you've been told is impossible. Each success, no matter how small, builds evidence for a new story.

6. Write Your Own Story

Literally. Write down the limiting belief, then write a new story about what's possible. Make it detailed, specific, and compelling. Read it regularly until it feels truer than the old limitation.

The Power of "What If They're Wrong?"

One of the most liberating questions you can ask yourself is: "What if they're wrong?" What if the teacher who said you weren't smart enough was wrong? What if the doctor who gave you a dire prognosis was wrong? What if the parent who said you'd never amount to anything was wrong?

What if their limitations weren't your limitations? What if their fears weren't your destiny? What if their assessment of your potential was based on incomplete information?

This question opens space for possibilities. It allows you to consider that maybe, just maybe, the story you've been living isn't the only story available to you.

Releasing the Power of Others' Opinions

Here's the truth: someone else's opinion of you is none of your business. It's their opinion, based on their perspective, filtered through their experiences, shaped by their limitations. It says more about them than it does about you.

But we give others' opinions tremendous power over our lives. We let them dictate our choices, limit our dreams, and define our possibilities. We treat their assessments like facts and their predictions like prophecies.

How to Release Others' Power Over Your Journey:

Remember that opinions are not facts. Even expert opinions are still opinions. They're educated guesses based on available information, but they're not guarantees.

Consider the source. Is this person speaking from expertise or fear? From love or limitation? From possibility or experience?

Trust your inner knowing. You know yourself better than anyone else knows you. You know your capacity for growth, your willingness to work, your ability to overcome obstacles.

Focus on what you can control. You can't control others' opinions, but you can control your response to them. You can choose whether to internalize them or investigate them.

Surround yourself with believers. Find people who see your potential, not just your limitations. Seek out voices that encourage expansion, not contraction.

The Difference Between Wisdom and Limitation

Not all advice is limited, and not all limitations are lies. Sometimes, people give us valuable guidance that saves us time, energy, or heartache. The key is learning to distinguish between wisdom and limitation.

Wisdom usually comes with options, alternatives, or ways to overcome obstacles. It acknowledges challenges while still believing in possibilities.

Limitation is definitive, absolute, and closes off possibilities. It says "never" instead of "not yet" and "impossible" instead of "difficult."

Wisdom empowers you to make informed decisions.

Limitation makes decisions for you.

Wisdom prepares you for challenges.

Limitation convinces you not to try.

Creating Your Own Authority

The most powerful thing you can do is become your own authority. This doesn't mean ignoring all advice or thinking you know everything. It means developing the ability to evaluate information, consider multiple perspectives, and make decisions based on your own values, goals, and inner knowing.

You become your own authority by:

- Developing critical thinking skills
- Seeking multiple opinions before making major decisions
- Learning to trust your intuition
- Taking responsibility for your choices
- Learning from your experiences
- Building confidence through action

The Miracle of Second Opinions

My story of having children despite medical predictions isn't unique. History is full of people who were told something was impossible and proved the experts wrong. People who were given death sentences and lived. People who were told they'd never walk again and ran marathons. People who were told they weren't smart enough and became leaders in their fields.

Sometimes, the second opinion that matters most is your own. Sometimes, the expert you need to trust is the one looking back at you in the mirror. Sometimes, the voice you need to listen to is the one that whispers, "what if" when everyone else is shouting "impossible."

Your Life, Your Story

As I watch my sons grow, these impossible boys who shouldn't exist according to medical expertise, I'm reminded daily that other people's opinions don't have to become our reality. Their limitations don't have to become our limitations. Their fears don't have to become our future.

You have the power to question every limiting belief you've ever been given. You have the right to challenge every "never" and "impossible" that's been declared over your life. You have the authority to write your own story, regardless of what anyone else says about your potential.

The experts in your life, teachers, doctors, parents, coaches, and employers, mean well. Most of them, anyway. But they're not the author of your story. They're not the architect of your destiny. They're not the final word on your possibilities. You are.

The Sound of Possibility

That sound my son made when he was born, those angry cries that sounded like "I'm mad!" was the sound of possibility breaking through limitation. It were the sound of life refusing to be contained by someone else's predictions, and the sound of a miracle announcing itself to a world that had declared it impossible.

What would your life sound like if you stopped believing the limitations others have placed on you? What would you attempt if you knew that expert opinions weren't divine decrees? What dreams would you pursue if you remembered that "never" is not a word that applies to your God-given potential?

The voice that told you that you couldn't, wouldn't, or shouldn't, who was that? And why did you believe them? More importantly, what are you going to do now that you know they might be wrong?

Your life is not bound by someone else's assessment of your potential. Your future is not limited by someone else's experience of what's possible. Your dreams are not invalid because someone else can't see them.

So, the next time someone tells you what you can't do, can't have, or can't become, remember my sons. Remember that medical expertise said they shouldn't exist, but they're upstairs right now, living their impossible lives.

Sometimes the most important thing you can do is prove the experts wrong. Your story is still being written, and you're the one holding the pen.

It's time to write a new story. One where your possibilities are bigger than their predictions. One where your potential is greater than their limitations. One where your dreams are more powerful than their doubts.

It's time to let your life make some noise. The beautiful, defiant sound of possibility breaking free from limitation. The sound of you refusing to be contained by someone else's version of what's possible.

X

CHAPTER 9: BOUNDARIES, BURNOUT & THE BOLDNESS TO SAY NO

"No" is a complete sentence. It doesn't need explanation, justification, or a five-page essay about why you can't do something. It doesn't need to be dressed up with excuses or softened with apologies. It's one of the most powerful words in language, and yet it's the hardest one for most of us to say.

We've been conditioned to believe that saying "yes" makes us helpful, valuable, and loved. We think that being available to everyone at all times makes us indispensable. We mistake being busy for being important, being overwhelmed for being needed.

If you don't learn to say "no" to some things, you'll never have the energy to say "yes" to the right things. If you don't protect your time and energy, nobody else will. If you don't set boundaries, people will assume you don't have any.

This chapter is about the life-changing power of boundaries. Not walls that keep people out, but fences that help you decide who and what gets access to your precious time and energy. It's about recognizing that burnout isn't a badge of honor, it's a warning sign. And it's about finding the boldness to disappoint some people so you can show up fully for the people and purposes that matter most.

The Myth of the Endless Yes

We live in a culture that celebrates the endless yes. The person who's always available, always helpful, always willing to take on one more task. We call them "team players," "go-getters," "high speed" and "dependable." We promote them, praise them, and point to them as examples of what good employees, soldiers, friends, and family members look like.

But what we don't talk about is the cost. The person who says yes to everything is often saying no to themselves. They're sacrificing their own goals, their own rest, their own relationships, their own dreams on the altar of other people's needs and expectations.

The endless yes looks like productivity, but it's actually a form of self-neglect. It looks like generosity, but it's often driven by fear of disappointing others, fear of being seen as selfish, fear of missing out, fear of not being needed.

I've learned that when you say yes to everything, your yes loses its power. When you're available to everyone, you're fully present for no one. When you have no boundaries, you have no sovereignty over your own life.

What Boundaries Are (And Aren't)

Let's clear up some misconceptions about boundaries, because I think this is where a lot of people get stuck.

Boundaries are not walls. They're not about shutting people out or becoming cold and unavailable. They're not about being mean, selfish, or uncaring.

Boundaries are fences. They're about being intentional about who and what gets access to your time, energy, and emotional bandwidth. They're about creating space for what matters most by saying no to what doesn't serve your highest good.

Think of boundaries like the property lines around your house. They don't mean you hate your neighbors or never want visitors. They just mean you get to decide who comes into your yard, when they come, and what they do while they're there.

Boundaries are:

- **Protective**, not punitive
- **Loving**, not limiting
- **Clear**, not cruel
- **Consistent**, not chaotic
- **About you**, not about controlling others

When you set a boundary, you're not trying to change someone else's behavior, you're defining your own. You're not saying, "You can't do that." You're saying, "I won't participate in that" or "I'm not available for that."

The Anatomy of Burnout

Burnout doesn't happen overnight. It's not like flipping a switch from "fine" to "completely overwhelmed." It's more like a slow leak in a tire. You might not notice at first, but eventually, you're running on a flat and wondering how you got there.

Burnout is what happens when you consistently give more than you have, when you operate from depletion instead of abundance, when you ignore your own needs while taking care of everyone else's.

The Early Warning Signs:

Physical symptoms: Chronic fatigue that sleep doesn't fix, frequent headaches, getting sick more often, changes in appetite or sleep patterns, feeling physically heavy or sluggish.

Emotional symptoms: Feeling overwhelmed by normal tasks, increased irritability, or impatience, feeling emotionally numb or disconnected, crying more easily or feeling like you might cry but can't.

Mental symptoms: Difficulty concentrating, forgetfulness, feeling scattered or unfocused, having trouble making decisions, feeling like your brain is in a fog.

Behavioral symptoms: Procrastinating on important tasks, withdrawing from social activities, increased use of alcohol, food, or other substances to cope, neglecting personal care or responsibilities.

Spiritual symptoms: Feeling disconnected from your purpose, questioning the meaning of your work or relationships, feeling spiritually empty or abandoned.

The Progression of Burnout:

Stage 1: The Honeymoon Phase - You're energized, committed, and willing to put in extra effort. You might work late, skip lunch, or say yes to additional responsibilities because you're motivated and capable.

Stage 2: The Onset of Stress - You start noticing that some days are more difficult than others. You might have occasional bad days, feel irritable sometimes, or notice that you're not sleeping as well.

Stage 3: Chronic Stress - The stress becomes more consistent. You're regularly tired, often irritable, and starting to see impacts on your work quality or relationships. You might get sick more often or feel like you're always behind.

Stage 4: Burnout - You're operating in survival mode. Everything feels overwhelming, you're emotionally exhausted, and you might feel cynical or detached from things that used to matter to you.

Stage 5: Habitual Burnout - This becomes your new normal. You've adapted to functioning at a depleted level, and you might not even remember what it felt like to have energy and enthusiasm.

The goal is to recognize the early warning signs and act before you reach the later stages. But even if you're already in Stage four or five, recovery is possible with intentional changes and often professional support.

The People Who Will Test Your Boundaries

When you start setting boundaries, you'll discover who in your life has been benefiting from your lack of them. These people will not be happy about your new limits, and they'll often try to push back.

The Guilt Tripper

"I can't believe you won't help me with this. I would do it for you." They make you feel selfish for having limits and use emotional manipulation to try to get you to change your mind.

How to handle them: Stay calm and don't take the bait. "I understand you're disappointed, but my decision stands." Don't justify or over-explain.

The Boundary Pusher

They'll keep asking after you've said no, hoping to wear you down. They might ask in different ways or at different times, thinking you'll eventually cave.

How to handle them: Be consistent. "As I mentioned before, I'm not available for that." Don't give them hope that your no might turn into a yes.

The Emergency Creator

Everything is urgent with this person. They lack planning skills and want you to bail them out of situations they could have avoided with better preparation.

How to handle them: Don't let someone else's poor planning become your emergency. "I'm sorry you're in a bind, but I'm not available to help with this."

The Minimizer

"It'll just take a few minutes." "It's not that hard." "Come on, it's no big deal." They try to make your boundaries seem unreasonable by downplaying what they're asking for.

How to handle them: "Whether it's five minutes or five hours, I'm not available right now."

The Guilt-by-Association Person

"What will people think?" "Your family is going to be so disappointed." They try to make you responsible for other people's reactions to your boundaries.

How to handle them: "I'm comfortable with my decision, and I'll handle any conversations that need to happen."

Remember: people who respect you will respect your boundaries. People who don't respect your boundaries don't respect you.

The Art of Saying No

Saying no is a skill, and like any skill, it gets easier with practice. But for most of us, especially women and people-pleasers, it feels incredibly uncomfortable at first.

Why We Struggle to Say No:

Fear of rejection: We worry that people won't like us if we're not always available.

Fear of missing out (FOMO): We think every opportunity is our last chance.

Guilt: We feel bad for not helping or not being available.

Lack of practice: We've never learned how to say no gracefully.

Conditioning: We've been taught that saying yes makes us good people.

Overestimating our capacity: We think we can handle more than we can.

Types of No:

Direct No: "No, I can't do that."

- Simple, clear, and requires no explanation

The Appreciate-But-Decline No: "I appreciate you thinking of me, but I can't take this on right now."

- Acknowledges the request while maintaining your boundary

Alternative No: "I can't do X, but I could do Y instead."

- Offers a compromise that works for you

Future No: "I'm not available now, but I might be able to help next month."

- Sets a boundary around timing

Referral No: "I can't help with this, but Sarah might be able to."

- Redirects the request to someone else

Partial No: "I can't take on the whole project, but I could help with the first part."

- Offers limited involvement

No Script:

When you're learning to say no, having a basic script can help:

1. **Acknowledge the request**: "Thank you for thinking of me..."
2. **Give your answer**: "...but I'm not available to help with this."
3. **Don't over-explain**: Resist the urge to justify your decision
4. **Offer an alternative if appropriate**: "I hope you find someone who can help."

What Not to Do When Saying No:

Don't lie: Making up elaborate excuses weakens your no and makes you feel bad about yourself.

Don't over-apologize: You don't need to be sorry for having boundaries.

Don't leave the door open: If you mean no, don't say "maybe" or "let me think about it."

Don't make it about the other person: Keep it about your capacity, not their worthiness.

Setting Boundaries in Different Areas of Life

Work Boundaries

Time boundaries: Clear start and end times for your workday, limited after-hours availability, protected time for focused work.

Communication boundaries: Designated times for checking email, limits on work-related calls or texts outside office hours.

Scope boundaries: Clear job descriptions, saying no to tasks outside your role without additional compensation or adjustment of other responsibilities.

Energy boundaries: Taking breaks, saying no to additional projects when you're at capacity, not working through lunch consistently.

Family Boundaries

Emotional boundaries: Not taking responsibility for family members' feelings or problems, limiting discussion of certain topics.

Time boundaries: Scheduled visits rather than drop-ins, limits on how often you're available for family crises.

Financial boundaries: Clear policies about lending money, not funding adult children's poor choices.

Holiday boundaries: Rotating celebrations, limiting travel, setting expectations about gifts or participation.

Friend Boundaries

Availability boundaries: Not being on call 24/7, having phone-free times, scheduling catch-ups rather than impromptu visits.

Emotional boundaries: Not being someone's only source of support, limiting conversations about certain topics.

Social boundaries: Choosing which events to attend, not feeling obligated to include everyone in everything.

Digital Boundaries

Social media boundaries: Limiting time spent scrolling, unfollowing accounts that make you feel bad, not engaging in arguments online.

Email boundaries: Designated times for checking email, not responding immediately to every message.

Phone boundaries: Putting your phone away during meals or family time, not answering calls during designated work or rest periods.

The Power of Protecting Your Energy

Your energy is not unlimited. You can't pour from an empty cup. These aren't just cute sayings, but the truth about human limitations that we ignore at our own peril.

Think of your energy like a bank account. Every yes is a withdrawal. Every boundary is a deposit. Every time you do something that drains you, you're spending your energy currency. Every time you do something that fills you up, you're making an investment in your future capacity.

Most people live in energy debt. They're constantly overdrawn, operating on fumes, wondering why they feel exhausted all the time. They've said yes to so many things that don't serve them that they have nothing left for the things that do.

Energy Drains vs. Energy Gains

Common Energy Drains:

- People who complain constantly but never take action
- Tasks that aren't aligned with your strengths or values
- Environments that are chaotic or negative
- Relationships that are one-sided
- Activities you do out of obligation rather than choice
- Perfectionism and overthinking
- Comparing yourself to others

- Saying yes when you mean no

Common Energy Gains:

- Time in nature
- Creative activities
- Physical movement that you enjoy
- Meaningful conversations
- Acts of service that align with your values
- Learning something new
- Time alone to recharge
- Celebrating small wins
- Saying no to things that don't serve you

Conducting an Energy Audit

Take a week to track your energy levels:

Morning: Rate your energy from 1-10 **Throughout the day**: Note what activities, people, or situations increase or decrease your energy **Evening**: Rate your energy again and reflect on what contributed to the changes

Look for patterns:

- What consistently drains your energy?
- What consistently boosts your energy?
- Are there energy drains you can eliminate or minimize?
- Are there energy gains you can increase?

The Seasons of Boundaries

Your boundaries don't have to be static. Just like the seasons change, your capacity and availability can change based on what's happening in your life.

Spring Season: Times of new beginnings, increased energy, and capacity for growth. You might be able to take on more during these seasons.

Summer Season: Times of high activity and productivity. You're in your element, but you need to be careful not to overcome yourself.

Fall Season: Times of harvest and preparation. You might need to start saying no to new commitments to focus on completing current projects.

Winter Season: Times of rest, reflection, and restoration. Your boundaries might be tighter as you focus on self-care and renewal.

Recognizing your seasons helps you set appropriate boundaries and manage expectations, both your own and others'.

Boundary Violations and How to Handle Them

Even with clear boundaries, people will sometimes cross them. How you respond when your boundaries are violated is just as important as setting them in the first place.

Common Boundary Violations:

- Showing up uninvited
- Continuing to ask after you've said no

- Going around you to get to someone else (like asking your spouse after you've declined)
- Making you feel guilty for having boundaries
- Ignoring your stated limits
- Using emotional manipulation to get you to change your mind

How to Respond:

Stay calm: Don't let emotion hijack your response. Take a breath and respond from a centered place.

Be direct: "We talked about this, and I said no. That hasn't changed."

Don't negotiate: Your boundaries aren't up for debate or discussion.

Follow through: If you said there would be consequences for boundary violations, enforce them.

Don't take it personally: Their inability to respect your boundaries is about them, not you.

When to Consider Ending Relationships:

If someone consistently violates your boundaries after you've clearly communicated them, you may need to consider whether this relationship is healthy for you. Relationships require mutual respect, and that includes respecting each other's limits.

This doesn't mean you have to cut people off for minor boundary issues, but it does mean you get to decide how much energy you want to invest in relationships with people who don't respect your limits.

The Guilt Factor

Let's talk about the elephant in the room: guilt. When you start setting boundaries, you're going to feel guilty. This is normal, expected, and temporary.

The guilt comes from years of conditioning that tells you that saying no is selfish, that your needs don't matter as much as others', that being a good person means being available to everyone all the time.

But here's the truth: guilt is not a reliable indicator of whether you're doing something wrong. Sometimes guilt is just the feeling you get when you're doing something different, something that goes against old patterns and expectations.

Healthy Guilt vs. Unhealthy Guilt

Healthy guilt happens when you've done something wrong or hurt someone. It motivates you to make amends and do better next time.

Unhealthy guilt happens when you haven't done anything wrong but feel bad anyway. It's often based on unrealistic expectations or conditioning that doesn't serve you.

When you feel guilty about setting a boundary, ask yourself:

- Have I actually done something wrong?
- Am I responsible for this person's reaction to my boundary?
- Would I want someone I care about to feel guilty for setting this same boundary?
- Is this guilt helping me or hurting me?

The Ripple Effect of Good Boundaries

When you start setting healthy boundaries, it doesn't just benefit you, it benefits everyone around you. Here's why:

You show up better: When you're not depleted and resentful, you can be more present and generous in your interactions.

You model healthy behavior: You show others that it's okay to have limits and take care of themselves.

You create more authentic relationships: People know that when you say yes, you mean it, and when you're present, you're fully there.

You reduce your stress: Lower stress means better health, better mood, and better decision-making.

You protect your priorities: By saying no to things that don't matter, you can say yes to things that do.

You teach people how to treat you: Clear boundaries communicate your values and expectations.

Practical Strategies for Boundary Setting

Start Small

You don't have to overhaul your entire life overnight. Start with one small boundary and practice maintaining it consistently.

Use the 24-Hour Rule

When someone asks you to do something, say, "Let me check my calendar and get back to you." This gives you time to think without the pressure of giving an immediate answer.

Practice Your No

Role-play with a trusted friend or practice in the mirror. The more you practice, the more natural it will feel.

Create Standard Responses

Have a few go-to phrases ready so you don't have to think on the spot:

- "I'm not available for that."
- "That doesn't work for me."
- "I'm not able to take that on right now."
- "I need to check my schedule and get back to you."

Set Up Systems

Use technology to help maintain boundaries:

- Set your phone to "Do Not Disturb" during certain hours
- Use email auto-responders to set expectations about response times
- Schedule social media time instead of mindlessly scrolling

Communicate Proactively

Don't wait for boundary violations to happen. Communicate your limits upfront:

- "I'm available for work calls between 9 AM and 6 PM."
- "I check email twice a day, at 10 AM and 3 PM."
- "I don't discuss work during family dinners."

When Boundaries Feel Selfish

One of the biggest obstacles to setting boundaries is the fear of being selfish. We've been taught that putting our needs first is wrong, that good people sacrifice themselves for others.

But here's a different perspective: taking care of yourself isn't selfish, it's self-preservation. You can't give what you don't have. You can't pour from an empty cup. You can't help others if you're drowning yourself.

Setting boundaries isn't about being selfish, it's about being sustainable. It's about creating a life that you can maintain long-term without burning out, getting resentful, or losing yourself in the process.

Think about it this way: if you don't take care of yourself, who will? If you don't protect your time and energy, who will? If you don't advocate for your own needs, who will?

The answer is no one. You are the only person who can set boundaries for your life. You are the only person who can decide what you're available for and what you're not. You are the only person who can protect your peace, your time, and your energy.

That's not selfish, that's responsible.

The Bold Art of Disappointing Others

Here's something that might sound shocking: you're going to disappoint people, and that's okay. In fact, it's necessary.
If you never disappoint anyone, it means you're saying yes to everything, which means you're probably disappointing the most important person in your life. You.

Disappointing others is not your problem to solve. Their disappointment is their emotion to manage. Your job is not to manage other people's feelings. Your job is to live your life in alignment with your values and priorities.

This doesn't mean you should be carelessly hurtful or dismiss others' feelings. It means you get to make choices that are right for you, even if those choices don't make everyone else happy.

The people who care about you will respect your boundaries, even if they're initially disappointed. The people who don't respect your boundaries are showing you that they care more about what you can do for them than they do about your well-being.

Recovery and Restoration

If you're reading this chapter and realizing you're already burned out, already overwhelmed, already operating from depletion, know that recovery is possible. It takes time, intentionality, and often support, but you can rebuild your energy and create a more sustainable way of living.

Steps for Recovery:

Assess the damage: How depleted are you? What areas of your life are suffering? What needs your immediate attention?

Get support: This might mean therapy, coaching, medical care, or just honest conversations with trusted friends or family members.

Start saying no: Begin declining new commitments while you focus on recovery.

Rest: Real rest, not just collapsing at the end of an overwhelming day. Intentional rest, restorative rest, guilt-free rest.

Reassess your commitments: What can you eliminate, delegate, or modify? What absolutely must stay, and what can go?

Rebuild slowly: As you start to feel better, add things back gradually and mindfully.

Learn the lesson: What led to burnout in the first place? What patterns need to change to prevent it from happening again?

Your Life, Your Rules

At the end of the day, this is your life. You get to decide how you spend your time, where you invest your energy, and what deserves your attention. You get to choose what you're available for and what you're not.

Setting boundaries isn't about being mean or selfish, it's about being intentional. It's about creating space for what matters most by saying no to what doesn't serve your highest good.

You don't need permission to have boundaries. You don't need to justify your limits to anyone. You don't need to apologize for taking care of yourself.

Your time is finite. Your energy is precious. Your peace is priceless. Protect them like the valuable resources they are.

The boldness of saying no to some things is what gives you the freedom to say yes to the right things. The courage to disappoint some people is what allows you to show up fully for the people who matter most.

Your boundaries are not walls but fences. They're not about keeping people out, they're about being intentional about who gets in.

They're not about being closed off, they're about being open to what serves your purpose and your peace.

So be bold. Set those boundaries. Say that no. Protect your energy. Disappoint some people. Choose yourself. Your future self will thank you for it.

And the people who truly care will respect you for it. Because at the end of the day, a life without boundaries is a life without direction. And a life without direction is not a life, it's just existence.

You deserve more than existence. You deserve a life that's intentional, purposeful, and aligned with your values.
You deserve boundaries.

→

CHAPTER 10: THE MIRROR AND THE MAP

There are two tools that will change your life if you learn to use them well: a mirror and a map. Not the literal ones sitting on your dresser or in your glove compartment, but the metaphorical ones that help you see where you are and figure out where you're going.

The mirror is self-reflection, the honest, sometimes uncomfortable practice of looking at yourself with clarity and compassion. It's about examining your patterns, your progress, your stumbles, and your growth without judgment, but with the intention to learn and improve.

The map is your personal roadmap for success. The dynamic, evolving plan that guides your decisions and helps you navigate toward your goals. It's not a rigid set of directions carved in stone, but a flexible guide that adjusts as you learn more about yourself and what you want from life.

Most people avoid the mirror because they're afraid of what they'll see. And most people skip the map because they think they don't need directions, they'll just figure it out as they go. But you can't get where you're going if you don't know where you are. And you can't improve what you don't examine.

This chapter is about the power of honest self-reflection and intentional planning. It's about learning to see yourself clearly so you can chart your course wisely. It's about the ongoing dance between reflection and action, between looking back to learn and looking forward to grow.

The Mirror: The Art of Honest Self-Reflection

Self-reflection gets a bad rap. People think it's narcissistic navel-gazing or an excuse to overthink everything. But real self-reflection isn't about getting stuck in analysis paralysis or beating yourself up for past mistakes. It's about developing self-awareness that makes growth possible.

Think of self-reflection like a GPS for your personal development. Your GPS doesn't judge you for taking a wrong turn. It just recalculates and gives you new directions. Self-reflection does the same thing. It helps you see where you are, understand how you got there, and figure out where to go next.

Reasons We Avoid Self-Reflection

Fear of what we'll find: We're afraid we'll discover things about ourselves that we don't like or don't want to face.

Shame about past decisions: We think reflection means dwelling on mistakes or regrets.

Perfectionism: We want to have it all figured out, so we avoid looking at areas where we're still growing.

Busyness: We stay so busy doing that we never take time for being or thinking.

Discomfort with stillness: Our culture celebrates constant motion, and reflection requires slowing down.

Fear of change: If we see clearly where we are, we might feel compelled to make changes we're not ready for.

But here's the truth: avoiding self-reflection doesn't make your problems go away, it just keeps you from seeing them clearly enough to solve them.

Components of Effective Self-Reflection

Honesty without brutality: Look at yourself clearly, but with compassion. You're trying to learn, not punish yourself.

Curiosity over judgment: Instead of asking "Why am I so stupid?" ask "What can I learn from this?"

Patterns over incidents: Look for recurring themes rather than isolated events. What keeps showing up in your life?

Growth over perfection: The goal isn't to become perfect, it's to become more self-aware and intentional.

Action over analysis: Reflection should lead to insight, and insight should lead to action.

Questions That Change Everything

The quality of your life is often determined by the quality of the questions you ask yourself. Here are some powerful questions for self-reflection:

About Your Current Reality:

- What patterns keep showing up in my life?
- What am I avoiding, and why?
- Where am I spending most of my time and energy?
- What's working well in my life right now?
- What's not working, and what role do I play in that?
- What stories am I telling myself about my circumstances?

About Your Growth:

- How have I changed in the last year?
- What have I learned about myself recently?
- Where have I been too comfortable, and where have I pushed myself?
- What skills or qualities do I want to develop?
- What feedback do I consistently receive from others?

About Your Values and Priorities:

- What matters most to me right now?
- Are my actions aligned with my stated values?
- What would I regret not doing or not being?
- If I had unlimited resources, how would I spend my time?

- What legacy do I want to leave?

About Your Relationships:

- What kind of friend/partner/family member am I?
- How do I show up in conflict?
- Where do I need to set better boundaries?
- Who brings out the best in me, and who brings out the worst?
- How do I contribute to the problems in my relationships?

About Your Goals and Dreams:

- Are my current goals still aligned with who I'm becoming?
- What am I pursuing out of genuine desire vs. external pressure?
- Where am I playing it too safe?
- What would I attempt if I knew I couldn't fail?
- What's one small step I could take today toward something I want?

The Different Types of Reflection

Daily Reflection (5-10 minutes)

End each day by asking yourself:

- What went well today?
- What could have gone better?
- What did I learn about myself?
- How do I want to show up tomorrow?

This isn't about perfection—it's about awareness and intentional improvement.

Weekly Reflection (15-30 minutes)

At the end of each week, look at the bigger picture:

- Did I make progress toward my goals this week?
- What patterns am I noticing in my days?
- Where did I feel most energized and alive?
- What do I want to do differently next week?

Monthly Reflection (30-60 minutes)

Once a month, take a deeper dive:

- How am I different than I was a month ago?
- What have I accomplished that I'm proud of?
- Where have I gotten stuck or off track?
- Do my goals still feel right, or do they need adjusting?
- What do I want to focus on in the coming month?

Quarterly Reflection (1-2 hours)

Every three months, do a comprehensive review:

- Am I living in alignment with my values?
- How have my priorities shifted?
- What relationships need attention?
- Where do I need to invest more time or energy?
- What do I need to let go of or say no to?

Annual Reflection (Half day or full day)

Once a year, take significant time to reflect on:

- Who have I become this year?
- What have been my biggest wins and biggest challenges?
- How have my goals and dreams evolved?

- What do I want to be different next year?
- What kind of person do I want to become?

The Map: Creating Your Personal Roadmap

A roadmap isn't a rigid set of directions, it's a flexible guide that helps you navigate toward your destination while allowing for detours, construction zones, and unexpected discoveries along the way.

Your personal roadmap should be dynamic, evolving as you learn more about yourself and what you want from life. It's not about having every step figured out, it's about having enough clarity to make good decisions and adjust to the course when needed.

Elements of an Effective Personal Roadmap

Vision: Where do you ultimately want to go? This is your big-picture destination, the life you're working toward.

Values: What principles will guide your journey? These are your non-negotiables, the things that matter most to you.

Goals: What specific outcomes do you want to achieve? These are your measurable milestones along the way.

Strategies: How will you achieve your goals? These are your plans of action, your chosen routes.

Systems: What daily/weekly/monthly practices will support your journey? These are your habits and routines.

Metrics: How will you know if you're on track? These are your check-in points and success indicators.

Flexibility: How will you adapt when things don't go according to plan? This is your contingency planning.

Step-by-Step: Building Your Roadmap

Step 1: Clarify Your Vision

Start with the end in mind. If you could fast-forward to the end of your life and look back, what would you want to see? What kind of person would you want to have been? What impact would you want to have made?

Your vision should be:

- **Inspiring**: It should energize and motivate you
- **Personal**: It should be yours, not what others expect of you
- **Specific enough to guide decisions**: Vague visions don't help much
- **Flexible enough to evolve**: You'll learn and grow along the way

Write your vision as if it's already happened: "I am..." rather than "I want to be..."

Step 2: Identify Your Core Values

Your values are your decision-making criteria. When you're faced with choices, your values help you decide which option aligns with who you want to be.

Common values include integrity, creativity, family, adventure, security, learning, service, freedom, connection, achievement, spirituality, justice, beauty, and fun.

Choose your top five to seven values and define what each one means to you specifically. For example, "integrity" might mean "being honest even when it's difficult" or "aligning my actions with my beliefs."

Step 3: Set Goals That Matter

Based on your vision and values, what specific goals will move you in the right direction? Your goals should be:

- **Aligned with your vision**: They should be stepping stones toward your bigger picture
- **Consistent with your values**: They shouldn't require you to compromise what matters most
- **Challenging but achievable**: They should stretch you without breaking you
- **Specific and measurable**: You should know when you've achieved them
- **Time-bound**: They should have deadlines to create urgency

Consider goals in different areas:

- Career/professional development
- Relationships/family
- Health/wellness
- Personal growth/learning
- Financial/security
- Fun/recreation
- Service/contribution

Step 4: Develop Strategies

For each goal, brainstorm multiple strategies you could use to achieve it. Don't just pick one approach—have backup plans and alternative routes.

Ask yourself:

- What's worked for me in similar situations before?
- What resources do I have available?
- Who could help me or provide guidance?
- What obstacles am I likely to encounter, and how can I prepare for them?
- What's the fastest route vs. the most sustainable route?

Step 5: Create Supporting Systems

Goals are achieved through daily actions, and daily actions become sustainable through systems and habits.

For each goal, identify:

- What daily habits would support this goal?
- What weekly or monthly practices would keep me on track?
- What environmental changes would make success more likely?
- What tools or resources do I need?
- How will I track my progress?

Step 6: Build in Accountability and Review

Your roadmap isn't a "set it and forget it" document, it's a living guide that needs regular attention.

Decide:

- How often will you review your progress? (weekly, monthly, quarterly)
- Who will help keep you accountable?
- What metrics will you track?
- How will you celebrate milestones?
- When will you do major roadmap updates?

The Power of Regular Check-Ins

One of the biggest mistakes people make is creating goals and then forgetting about them. Life gets busy, priorities shift, and before you know it, you're working toward something that no longer serves you or ignoring something that could transform your life.

Regular check-ins with your goals and your roadmap are essential for several reasons:

They Keep You Connected to Your Why

When you regularly revisit your goals, you reconnect with the reasons you set them in the first place. This rekindling of purpose can reignite motivation when it starts to fade.

They Allow for Course Correction

Life rarely goes according to plan. Regular check-ins help you spot when you're drifting off course and adjust before you're completely lost.

They Help You Recognize Progress

We often focus so much on what we haven't achieved that we miss what we have accomplished. Regular reviews help you see and celebrate your progress.

They Reveal What's Not Working

If you're consistently missing targets in one area, regular check-ins help you identify whether you need to adjust your strategy, your timeline, or the goal itself.

They Support Learning and Growth

Each check-in is an opportunity to learn something about yourself, your patterns, your strengths, and your challenges.

Making Reflection and Planning Practical

Create a Reflection Ritual

Make self-reflection a regular practice by creating a ritual around it:

- **Choose a consistent time**: Maybe Sunday evenings for weekly reflection, the last day of each month for monthly reviews
- **Create a comfortable environment**: Find a quiet space where you won't be interrupted
- **Use prompts or questions**: Don't just sit and think—use specific questions to guide your reflection
- **Write it down**: There's something powerful about putting your thoughts on paper
- **Be consistent**: Even 10 minutes of regular reflection is more valuable than hours of sporadic thinking

Use Tools That Work for You

Everyone's different, so find reflection and planning tools that match your style:

- **Journaling**: Free-form writing about your thoughts and experiences
- **Structured templates**: Specific questions or frameworks to guide your thinking
- **Digital apps**: Tools like Day One, Journey, or even simple note-taking apps
- **Voice recordings**: If you're more of a verbal processor
- **Art or visual mapping**: If you're a visual learner, try mind maps or vision boards

Make It Sustainable

The best reflection practice is the one you'll actually do consistently:

- **Start small**: Better to reflect for 5 minutes regularly than 2 hours sporadically
- **Be realistic**: Don't commit to daily hour-long reflection sessions if you can barely find time for a shower
- **Focus on insight, not perfection**: The goal is learning, not having perfect answers
- **Adjust as needed**: If something isn't working, change it

Common Roadmap Mistakes and How to Avoid Them

Mistake #1: Making It Too Complicated

The problem: Creating elaborate planning systems that take more time to maintain than to actually work toward your goals.

The solution: Keep it simple. Your roadmap should clarify your path, not complicate it.

Mistake #2: Setting It and Forgetting It

The problem: Creating goals and never looking at them again until the end of the year when you realize you've accomplished none of them.

The solution: Build regular review sessions into your calendar and treat them as non-negotiable appointments.

Mistake #3: Being Too Rigid

The problem: Sticking to goals that no longer serve you because you don't want to admit you've changed your mind.

The solution: Remember that changing your goals isn't failing—it's growing. Your roadmap should evolve as you do.

Mistake #4: Focusing Only on Outcomes

The problem: Measuring success only by whether you achieved specific results, ignoring the growth and learning that happened along the way.

The solution: Track both outcome goals and process goals. Celebrate effort and improvement, not just final results.

Mistake #5: Going It Alone

The problem: Trying to stay accountable to yourself without any external support or accountability.

The solution: Share your goals with people who will support and challenge you. Consider working with a coach, mentor, or accountability partner.

The Integration of Mirror and Map

The mirror and the map work best when they're used together. Self-reflection without planning leads to insight without action. Planning without reflection leads to action without learning. Here's how they work together:

Reflection informs planning: What you learn about yourself through reflection should influence your goals, strategies, and systems.

Planning gives direction to reflection: Having clear goals gives you specific things to reflect on—what's working, what isn't, what needs to adjust.

Both support growth: Reflection helps you understand where you are and how you got there. Planning helps you decide where to go and how to get there.

Both require honesty: Just as reflection requires honest self-assessment, effective planning requires honest assessment of your resources, constraints, and capabilities.

Both are ongoing processes: Neither reflection nor planning is a one-time activity, they're lifelong practices that evolve as you do.

When Reflection Gets Difficult

Sometimes self-reflection reveals things we don't want to see. Maybe you realize you've been pursuing someone else's dream instead of your own. Maybe you discover patterns of behavior that are holding you back. Maybe you acknowledge that you've been avoiding something important out of fear.

These difficult realizations are gifts, even though they don't feel like it at the time. They're opportunities to make changes that could transform your life. But they're only gifts if you receive them with curiosity rather than self-judgment.

When Reflection Reveals Uncomfortable Truths:

Acknowledge without judgment: "I notice that I consistently procrastinate on important tasks" rather than "I'm so lazy and undisciplined."

Look for patterns, not just incidents: What's the deeper issue behind the surface behavior?

Consider the function: What need was this behavior meeting? How can you meet that need in a healthier way?

Focus on learning: What does this teach you about yourself? How can you use this information to make better choices?

Act: Insight without action is just interesting information. What will you do differently based on what you've learned?

The Gift of Self-Awareness

The combination of regular self-reflection and intentional planning creates something powerful: self-awareness. And self-awareness is the foundation of all growth, all change, all meaningful achievements.

When you know yourself well, incuding your strengths and weaknesses, your patterns and triggers, your values, and motivations, you can make better decisions. You can choose goals that fit your life instead of goals that look good on paper. You can identify obstacles before they derail you. You can celebrate progress in ways that matter to you.

Self-awareness helps you:

- **Make better decisions** because you understand your own biases and tendencies
- **Set better boundaries** because you know what drains your energy and what fills it
- **Choose better relationships** because you know what you need and what you can offer
- **Pursue better goals** because you understand what actually motivates you
- **Handle challenges better** because you know your own resilience patterns
- **Enjoy life more** because you're living authentically instead of performing for others

Your Reflection and Planning Practice

As we wrap up this chapter, I want to challenge you to start your own reflection and planning practice. You don't need to do everything at once. Start small and build from there.

This Week:

Choose one evening this week for a 20-minute reflection session. Ask yourself:

- What went well this week?
- What was challenging?
- What did I learn about myself?
- How do I want to approach next week differently?

This Month:

Set aside 30-60 minutes for a deeper reflection and planning session:

- Review your current goals, do they still feel right?
- Identify one area where you want to grow or improve
- Create a simple plan for making progress in that area
- Schedule your next monthly check-in

This Quarter:

Block out a few hours for a comprehensive review:

- Reflect on your growth over the past three months
- Assess your progress toward your major goals
- Identify what's working well and what needs to change
- Set intentions for the next quarter

This Year:

Plan an annual retreat with you even if it's just a few hours at a coffee shop:

- Celebrate your growth and achievements from the past year
- Reflect on the lessons you've learned
- Clarify your vision and values
- Set goals and create plans for the coming year

The Journey of Becoming

The mirror and the map aren't just tools for achieving goals, they're instruments for becoming who you're meant to be. They help you navigate the ongoing journey of growth, change, and self-discovery that is a life well-lived.

Regular self-reflection keeps you honest about where you are and how you got there. Intentional planning keeps you moving toward where you want to go. Together, they create a powerful cycle of learning and growing that can transform not just what you achieve, but who you become in the process.

Remember, you are both the traveler and the guide on this journey. You get to choose your destination, chart your course, and decide what kind of person you want to be along the way. But you can only make these choices wisely if you're willing to look honestly at where you are and plan thoughtfully for where you're going.

The mirror shows you the truth of who you are right now, not to judge or criticize, but to understand and learn. The map shows you the possibility of who you could become—not to pressure or overwhelm, but to inspire and guide. Both are necessary. Both are gifts. Both are waiting for you to use them.

So, look in the mirror. Not the one that shows you your reflection, but the one that shows you your patterns, your growth, your possibilities. What do you see?

And pull out your map. Not the one that shows you streets and highways, but the one that shows you your values, your goals, your dreams. Where do you want to go?

The journey of becoming who you're meant to be starts with knowing where you are and deciding where you want to go. The mirror and the map will help you do both.

X

Chapter 11: The Journey Is Ugly, Beautiful, and Yours

Your journey will not look like a motivational poster. It won't be a steady upward climb with perfect lighting and inspirational quotes floating in the background. It won't be a straight line from Point A to Point B, and it won't be Instagram-worthy every step of the way.

Your journey will be messy. It will be inconsistent. It will be full of contradictions, moments of soaring confidence followed by crushing self-doubt, periods of clear direction followed by total confusion, times of rapid progress followed by what feels like endless plateaus.

There will be days when you feel like you're crushing it, like you've finally figured out the secret to life, like you're unstoppable. And there will be days when you feel like you're failing at everything, like you have no idea what you're doing, like you should just give up and become a professional couch potato.

Both kinds of days are part of your journey. Both are necessary. Both are beautiful in their own way, even when they don't feel like it.

This chapter is about accepting the imperfect, contradictory, gloriously human nature of your path. It's about learning to embrace the beauty and struggle, victories and setbacks, clarity and confusion. It's about understanding that your journey doesn't have to be perfect to be meaningful, and it doesn't have to be pretty to be powerful.

Most importantly, it's about remembering that this journey, with all its ups and downs, twists and turns, beautiful moments, and ugly crying sessions, is yours. It's uniquely, authentically, irreplaceably yours.

The Myth of the Perfect Journey

Social media has ruined us. We see highlight reels and think they're documentaries. We see someone's carefully curated "Day in My Life" posts and think that's what their actual life looks like 24/7. We see the victory posts and forget about all the failures that came before them.

We've been sold a lie about what pursuing your dreams looks like. The myth says it should be:

- Constantly inspiring
- Steadily progressive
- Visually appealing

- Always meaningful
- Perpetually motivated
- Consistently confident

But the reality is that most of the time, pursuing your dreams looks like:

- Showing up when you don't feel like it
- Making progress so slow it's barely visible
- Doing unsexy work that no one sees
- Questioning whether any of it matters
- Pushing through when motivation is nowhere to be found
- Acting confident while feeling completely uncertain

The myth of the perfect journey is dangerous because it makes us think we're doing something wrong when our experience doesn't match the fantasy. We start to believe that struggle means we're not cut out for this, that setbacks mean we should quit, that confusion means we're on the wrong path.

The struggle is not a sign that you're doing it wrong. The struggle is a sign that you're doing something that matters. The setbacks are not proof that you should quit. They're proof that you're taking risks and pushing boundaries. The confusion is not evidence that you're on the wrong path. It's evidence that you're growing beyond your current understanding.

Beauty in the Ugly

There's something beautiful about the ugly parts of your journey, even though you might not see it while you're in them. The beauty is in the raw humanity of it all—the fact that you're brave enough to try, vulnerable enough to fail, and resilient enough to keep going.

Not knowing what comes next means you're not playing it safe. You're not staying in the comfortable bubble of predictability. You're venturing into unknown territory, which is the only place where growth and discovery happen.

Uncertainty is uncomfortable, but it's also where possibility lives. When you don't know what's coming, anything could happen. That's terrifying and thrilling at the same time.

Failure means you tried something that mattered enough to risk falling short. It means you stretched beyond your comfort zone. It means you chose courage over comfort, growth over safety. Every failure is data. Every setback is information. Every mistake is a teacher. The people who never fail are the people who never try anything worth failing at.

Struggle means you're doing something difficult, something that requires growth, something that's transforming you. Easy things don't change us. Comfortable things don't challenge us. Struggle is the price of becoming who you're meant to be.

The struggle is also what makes victories meaningful. The sweetest success is the one that comes after the most difficult journey. The most precious achievements are the ones that cost you something.

Confusion means you're grappling with something complex, something that doesn't have easy answers. It means you're thinking deeply, questioning assumptions, exploring possibilities.

Confusion is often the precursor to breakthrough. When you're confused, you're on the edge of understanding something new. You're in the space between what you used to know and what you're about to discover.

Slow progress means you're building something sustainable, something with deep roots. Fast progress is exciting, but slow progress is often more lasting.

Slow progress teaches patience, persistence, and the value of small steps. It builds character in a way that instant success never could. It makes you appreciate the journey, not just the destination.

The Seasons of Your Journey

Your journey, like the natural world, has seasons. Each season has its own beauty, its own challenges, and its own purpose. Understanding these seasons can help you navigate them with more grace and less resistance.

Spring: The Season of New Beginnings

This is when you're starting something new, planting seeds, full of hope and possibility. Everything feels fresh and exciting. You have energy, optimism, and big dreams.

The beauty: The excitement of new possibilities, the energy of fresh starts, the hope of what could be.

The challenges: Impatience for results, unrealistic expectations, not knowing what you're doing yet.

How to navigate it: Enjoy the energy while it lasts. Plant lots of seeds. Don't expect immediate results. Focus on learning and building foundations.

Summer: The Season of Growth and Action

This is when you're in full swing, making progress, seeing results. You know what you're doing, you have momentum, and things are happening.

The beauty: Visible progress, increased confidence, the satisfaction of hard work paying off.

The challenges: Burnout from too much activity, losing sight of the bigger picture, getting overwhelmed by success.

How to navigate it: Pace yourself. Remember to rest. Stay connected to your why. Don't let success go to your head.

Fall: The Season of Harvest and Reflection

This is when you're reaping what you've sown, celebrating achievements, and preparing for what's next. You can see how far you've come and appreciate the journey.

The beauty: Seeing the fruits of your labor, gaining wisdom from experience, feeling proud of your growth.

The challenges: Fear of losing what you've gained, uncertainty about what comes next, pressure to maintain success.

How to navigate it: Celebrate your wins. Reflect on what you've learned. Prepare for the next season without clinging to this one.

Winter: The Season of Rest and Renewal

This is when things slow down, when you're not seeing much visible progress, when you might feel stuck or dormant. It can feel like nothing is happening.

The beauty: Time for rest and reflection, opportunity to go deeper, preparation for the next growth cycle.

The challenges: Feeling like you're not making progress, losing motivation, wondering if you should quit.

How to navigate it: Embrace the rest. Use this time for reflection and planning. Trust that growth is happening beneath the surface.

All seasons are necessary. You can't have constant summer. You can't skip winter and go straight to spring. Each season serves a purpose in your growth and development.

The Highs and Lows of Meaningful Living

Pursuing a meaningful life that aligned with your values, dreams, and purpose, is not a path of constant happiness. In fact, it might involve more emotional ups and downs than a "safe" life would. But the lows are worth it because they're the price of the highs.

The Highs

Moments of clarity when everything makes sense and you know exactly what you're supposed to be doing.

Breakthrough moments when you accomplish something you didn't think was possible.

Connection with purpose when you feel deeply aligned with your why and know that your work matters.

Growth celebrations when you recognize how far you've come and who you've become in the process.

Impact moments when you see how your journey has affected others in positive ways.

Flow states when you're so engaged in what you're doing that time disappears and everything feels effortless.

The Lows

Imposter syndrome when you feel like you don't belong or don't deserve your success.

Comparison spirals when you look at others' journeys and feel like you're falling behind.

Motivation deserts when you can't remember why you started or why you should continue.

Failure hangovers when setbacks leave you questioning everything about your path.

Loneliness when you feel like no one understands what you're going through.

Overwhelmed when the gap between where you are and where you want to be feels impossibly wide.

Both the highs and the lows are part of the package. You can't have one without the other. The depth of your lows often corresponds to the height of your highs. The people who feel the most joy are often the ones who've experienced the most pain.

Why Your Journey Looks Different

Your journey will not look like your friend's journey, your sibling's journey, your mentor's journey, or the journey of that person you follow on social media. This is not a problem to be solved. It's a feature of human experience.

You're not starting from the same place as anyone else. You have different advantages, different challenges, different resources, different constraints. Your family background, your education, your life experiences, your personality, your circumstances, all of these factors influence your journey.

Even if you and someone else have similar goals, you're not going to the exact same place. Your version of success will be different from theirs. Your definition of fulfillment will be personal to you.

You have different amounts of time, money, energy, and support available to you. You have different skills, different connections, different opportunities. These differences will shape how your journey unfolds.

Some people are early bloomers, others are late bloomers. Some people move quickly, others move slowly. Some people take linear paths, others take scenic routes. There's no universal timeline for success or growth.

You're going to face challenges that are unique to your situation, your personality, your circumstances. The obstacles that derail someone else might not even slow you down, while challenges that you struggle with might be easy for others.

You have unique gifts, talents, and abilities that will make your journey distinctly yours. The way you solve problems, the way you connect with others, the way you see the world, these are your superpowers, and they'll show up in your journey in ways that are uniquely yours.

Embracing the Paradoxes

Your journey will be full of contradictions and paradoxes. Instead of trying to resolve them or make them make sense, learn to embrace them. Life is paradoxical, and your journey is life.

Often at the same time. You can feel confident about your abilities while feeling insecure about your worthiness. You can be sure about your direction while being uncertain about your decisions.

You can be deeply grateful for how far you've come while still feeling dissatisfied with where you are. Gratitude and ambition can coexist.

You'll want to quit and keep going. Sometimes at the same time. The desire to quit doesn't mean you should quit. The desire to keep going doesn't mean it will always be easy.

You can have people who love and support you while still feeling alone on your journey. Some parts of your path only you can walk.

You can be making objective progress while feeling subjectively stuck. Growth isn't always visible, especially to the person doing the growing.

You have the power to choose your responses, your actions, your attitudes. You don't have the power to control outcomes, other people, or circumstances.

The Art of Embracing It All

Embracing your journey, the beautiful parts and the ugly parts, is not about pretending everything is fine or forcing yourself to be positive all the time. It's about accepting that this is what it looks like to be human, to grow, to pursue something meaningful.

Acceptance doesn't mean resignation. It means acknowledging what it is without wasting energy fighting reality. You can accept that you're struggling while still working to improve your situation.

Every experience, positive or negative, has something to teach you. The question isn't whether you'll face challenges, it's what you'll learn from them.

Don't wait for major milestones to celebrate. Acknowledge the small victories, the tiny steps forward, the moments of growth. These are the building blocks of your journey.

Your feelings are valid and important. Don't rush to fix or change them. Let yourself feel what you feel, then ask what the emotion is trying to tell you.

Talk to yourself the way you would talk to a good friend. You're doing the best you can with what you have. You're human, and humans are imperfect.

When the journey gets difficult, reconnect with your deeper purpose. Why did you start this path? What matters to you? What are you working toward?

You don't have to see the whole staircase to take the first step. You don't have to understand everything to keep moving forward. Trust that the journey is unfolding as it should.

The Gifts Hidden in the Struggle

The difficult parts of your journey aren't just obstacles to overcome—they're gifts in disguise. They're opportunities to develop qualities that can't be developed any other way.

Resilience

You can't build resilience without facing challenges. Every time you get knocked down and get back up, you're strengthening your ability to handle future difficulties.

Empathy

Your struggles help you understand and connect with others who are going through similar challenges. Your pain becomes your ability to help others.

Humility

Setbacks and failures keep you grounded. They remind you that you're human, that you don't have all the answers, that you're still learning and growing.

Gratitude

When you've experienced real difficulty, you don't take the good times for granted. You appreciate what you have because you know what it's like to not have it.

Wisdom

This is different from knowledge. Knowledge tells you a tomato is a fruit. Wisdom tells you not to put them in a fruit salad. Experience, both positive and negative, gives you wisdom that can't be gained through books or advice. You learn things about yourself, about life, about what really matters.

Strength

Not physical strength, but inner strength. The strength to keep going when things get hard. The strength to believe in yourself when others don't. The strength to stay true to your path even when it's difficult.

Compassion

For you and others. When you've struggled, you understand that everyone is fighting battles you can't see. You become more patient, more understanding, more kind.

Your Journey Is Enough

In a world that constantly tells you to do more, be more, achieve more, it's radical to believe that your journey—exactly as it is—is enough. You don't have to prove anything to anyone. You don't have to justify your path or your pace. You don't have to make your journey look like anyone else's.

Your journey is enough because it's yours. It's the path that's teaching you what you need to learn, growing you in the ways you need to grow, taking you where you need to go. It's not perfect, but it's perfect for you.

Your struggles are not a sign that you're doing it wrong, they're a sign that you're doing something real. Your setbacks are not proof that you should quit—they're proof that you're trying something that matters. Your confusion is not evidence that you're lost, it's evidence that you're exploring uncharted territory.

The Beauty of Owning Your Story

When you fully embrace your journey—the whole messy, beautiful, imperfect thing—you reclaim your power. You stop trying to make your story look like someone else's story. You stop apologizing for your path. You stop waiting for permission to be proud of how far you've come.

Owning your story means:

- Celebrating your wins, even the small ones
- Acknowledging your growth, even when it's hard to see
- Being honest about your struggles without being defined by them
- Sharing your experience to help others who might be going through similar challenges
- Refusing to let anyone else write your narrative
- Trusting that your journey is unfolding exactly as it should

Your story is not a tragedy because it includes difficult chapters. Your story is not less valuable because it doesn't look like someone else's. Your story is not incomplete because you're still writing it.

The Journey Continues

As we wrap up this chapter, I want you to remember that your journey is not a destination to reach. It's a path to walk. There's no finish line where you'll suddenly have it all figured out, where the struggles will end, where everything will be perfect.

The journey continues. And that's the point.

You will keep growing. You will keep learning. You will keep evolving. You will keep facing new challenges and discovering new strengths. You will keep surprising yourself with what you're capable of.

Some days will be beautiful. Some days will be ugly. Most days there will be a mixture of both. All of them will be yours. So, embrace it all. The victories and the defeats. The clarity and the confusion. The progress and the setbacks. The joy and the sorrow. The beauty and the struggle.

This is your journey. It's not perfect, but it's perfectly yours. And that's more than enough.

It's everything.

CHAPTER 12: DON'T WAIT FOR PERMISSION

Nobody is coming to give you permission to live your life.

Not your parents, not your boss, not your friends, not your spouse, not your children, not society, not the government. Nobody is going to tap you on the shoulder and say, "You have our official approval to pursue your dreams now."

You're waiting for permission that's never coming from people who don't have the authority to give it.

You have to understand that you don't need permission to be who you are, to want what you want, to dream what you dream, or to go after what matters to you. You never did. The only person whose permission you need is the one looking back at you in the mirror.

This chapter is about taking ownership of your dreams without waiting for external approval. It's about making bold moves without needing validation from others. It's about recognizing that you are the expert of your own life, the author of your own story, and the CEO of your own existence.

It's time to stop asking for permission and start taking ownership.

The Permission Trap

From the moment we're born, we're conditioned to seek permission. We ask permission to go to the bathroom, to speak, to leave the table, to play with friends. This makes sense when we're children. We need guidance, structure, and protection.

But somewhere along the way, many of us never learned to give ourselves permission. We got stuck in that childhood pattern of waiting for someone else to tell us it's okay to want what we want, to be who we are, to pursue what we're passionate about.

The permission trap looks like:

- Waiting for your parents to approve of your career choice
- Needing your friends to validate your relationship decisions
- Seeking your boss's blessing before pursuing a side hustle
- Requiring society's acceptance before expressing your authentic self
- Wanting your family's support before making a major change
- Needing experts to confirm that your idea is viable before trying it

The problem with the permission trap is that you're giving your power away. You're making other people responsible for your life decisions.

You're treating yourself like a child who can't be trusted to make choices about your own existence.

Why We Get Stuck Seeking Permission

Fear of disapproval: We're afraid that if we act without permission, people won't like us or will judge us harshly.

Fear of responsibility: If someone else gives us permission, they share responsibility for the outcome. If we give ourselves permission, we're fully accountable.

Learned helplessness: We've been conditioned to believe that other people know better than we do about our own lives.

Imposter syndrome: We don't feel qualified to make decisions about our own path.

Conflict avoidance: Seeking permission feels safer than potentially upsetting people by acting independently.

Cultural conditioning: Some cultures emphasize collective decision-making and family approval over individual autonomy.

The Authority You've Been Looking For

Here's the truth that might be hard to accept: the authority you've been seeking outside yourself has been inside you all along.

You are the world's leading expert on your own life. You know your circumstances, your constraints, your dreams, your values, your capacity, your history, your motivations better than anyone else ever could.

Yes, other people can offer wisdom, guidance, and perspective. Yes, you should seek advice from people who have experience in areas where you don't. Yes, you should consider how your decisions affect the people you love.

But at the end of the day, you're the one who has to live with your choices. You're the one who has to wake up with your life every morning. You're the one who has to answer to yourself about whether you're living authentically and pursuing what matters to you.

You Are Qualified to Make Decisions About Your Life Because:

You know your values better than anyone else: What matters to you, what you stand for, what you won't compromise on.

You understand your circumstances: The full context of your situation, your resources, your constraints, your opportunities.

You know your capacity: What you can manage, what energizes you, what drains you, what you're capable of learning.

You understand your motivation: What drives you, what scares you, what excites you, what fulfills you.

You know your history: What you've overcome, what you've learned, how you've grown, what patterns you need to break.

You have access to your intuition: That inner knowing that can't be quantified but is often the most dependable guide you have.

Taking Ownership of Your Dreams

Taking ownership of your dreams means shifting from "Can I?" to "How will I?" It means moving from seeking permission to making plans. It means transitioning from asking others what they think to asking yourself what you want.

What Dream Ownership Looks Like:

You stop explaining yourself endlessly: You don't need to justify your dreams to anyone. You can share them, but you don't need approval for them to be valid.

You make decisions based on your values, not others' expectations: Your choices align with what matters to you, not what would make others happy.

You act before you feel ready: You don't wait for perfect conditions or complete certainty. You start where you are with what you have.

You manage criticism without abandoning your path: You can listen to feedback without letting it derail your dreams.

You celebrate your wins without needing external validation: Your achievements matter because they matter to you, not because others recognize them.

You trust your instincts: You value your inner guidance as much as (or more than) external advice.

The Shift from Permission-Seeking to Dream Ownership:

Instead of: "Do you think I should start my own business?" **Try**: "I'm starting my own business. What advice do you have for someone in my situation?"

Instead of: "Is it okay if I go back to school?" **Try**: "I've decided to go back to school. Can you help me figure out the logistics?"

Instead of: "Would it be selfish of me to pursue this opportunity?"
Try: "This opportunity aligns with my goals. How can I pursue it responsibly?"

Instead of: "Do you think I'm too old/young/inexperienced to try this?" **Try**: "I'm going to try this. What do I need to learn or prepare for?"

Notice the difference? In the first examples, you're asking for permission. In the second example, you're asking for support with a decision you've already made.

Practical Tips for Making Bold Moves

Making bold moves without external validation requires courage, but it also requires strategy. Here are practical ways to give yourself permission and take ownership of your dreams:

1. Start with Small Acts of Self-Permission

You don't have to start with life-changing decisions. Practice giving yourself permission in small ways:

- Take a different route to work because you want to see something new
- Try a restaurant you've been curious about
- Sign up for a class that interests you
- Speak up in a meeting when you have an idea
- Wear something that makes you feel confident
- Say no to something you don't want to do

These small acts build your permission-giving muscle.

2. Create Your Own Advisory Board

Instead of waiting for one person to give you permission, create a diverse group of advisors whose perspectives you value. This might include:

- A mentor in your field
- A trusted friend who knows you well
- Someone who's made a similar transition
- A professional coach or counselor
- Someone whose judgment you respect

Seek their input, but remember that you're gathering information, not waiting for approval.

3. Use the "What Would I Advise a Friend?" Test

When you're struggling to give yourself permission, imagine a close friend came to you with your exact situation. What would you tell them? Often, we're much more generous and encouraging with others than we are with ourselves.

4. Set Permission Deadlines

Give yourself a deadline for seeking input, then commit to deciding by that date regardless of whether you've received the validation you're seeking. This prevents you from staying stuck in analysis paralysis forever.

5. Practice the "Minimum Viable Permission" Approach

Instead of waiting for enthusiastic approval from everyone, look for the minimum viable permission you need to move forward.

Maybe you don't need your parents to be thrilled about your career change, maybe you just need them to not actively sabotage it.

6. Separate Information from Permission

Learn to distinguish between seeking information (which is often helpful) and seeking permission (which can keep you stuck).

Seeking information sounds like: "What should I know about starting a business?" "What challenges did you face when you made this transition?" "What resources would you recommend?"

Seeking permission sounds like: "Do you think I should start a business?" "Is this a good idea?" "Would you do this if you were me?"

7. Create Your Own Validation Systems

Don't wait for others to celebrate your wins or acknowledge your progress. Create systems to validate yourself:

- Keep a list of your accomplishments
- Celebrate small wins with something you enjoy
- Write encouraging notes yourself
- Take progress photos or keep a journal
- Share your wins with people who will celebrate with you

8. Practice the "I'm Going to Try" Mindset

Instead of asking "Should I?" start saying "I'm going to try." This shifts you from seeking permission to taking experimental action. You can always adjust course based on what you learn.

9. Identify Your Permission Patterns

Notice when and from whom you tend to seek permission. Is it your parents? Your spouse? Your friends? Your boss? Social media?

Understanding your patterns helps you recognize when you're doing it and choose differently.

10. Remember That Regret Goes Both Ways

We often worry about regretting action, but we should also consider the regret of inaction. What will you regret more: trying something and it not working out, or never trying it at all?

Why Others Can't Give You Permission

Even if people wanted to give you permission to pursue your dreams, they literally can't. Here's why:

They Don't Have Complete Information

No one else has access to all the information about your life, your full history, your complete circumstances, your inner motivations, your capacity for growth, your tolerance for risk. They're making recommendations based on incomplete data.

They're Filtered Through Their Own Experience

When people give you advice, they're filtering it through their own experiences, fears, limitations, and beliefs. What feels impossible to them might be completely achievable for you.

They Don't Have to Live with the Consequences

You're the one who has to live with your choices. Other people can give advice from a safe distance, but you're the one who has to deal with the daily reality of your decisions.

They Can't Account for Your Growth Potential

Other people see you as you are now, but they can't fully account for how you might grow, what you might learn, or how you might rise to meet challenges. You have growth potential that others can't measure.

Their Approval Doesn't Change Reality

Someone else's blessing doesn't make your dreams more valid or more likely to succeed. Someone else's disapproval doesn't make your dreams less worthy or less achievable.

They Have Their Own Agendas

Sometimes people withhold permission not because they don't believe in you, but because your growth or change threatens their comfort zone. They might benefit from keeping you small or staying in your current role.

The Cost of Waiting for Permission

While you're waiting for permission that may never come, life is happening. Opportunities are passing. Time is ticking. Your dreams are on hold while you seek approval from people who may never give it.

What You Miss While Waiting:

Learning opportunities: Every day you don't start is a day you don't learn what you need to know.

Growth experiences: The person you become by pursuing your dreams is different from the person you are while waiting for permission.

Momentum: Action creates momentum, but waiting creates stagnation.

Connections: When you're actively pursuing your dreams, you meet people and create relationships that support your journey.

Discovery: You can't discover what's possible until you start trying.

Time: This is the big one. Time is the one resource you can't get back. Every day you wait is a day you could have been building toward your dreams.

The Hidden Costs:

Resentment: Waiting for permission can create resentment toward the people whose approval you're seeking.

Regret: The regret of not trying can be more painful than the regret of trying and failing.

Decreased self-trust: The longer you wait for external validation, the less you trust your own judgment.

Missed timing: Some opportunities are time sensitive. Waiting too long can mean missing your window.

Energy drain: Seeking permission requires emotional energy that could be used for action.

When Others Don't Support Your Dreams

Not everyone is going to support your dreams. Some people might actively discourage you. This doesn't mean your dreams are wrong, it often means your dreams make other people uncomfortable.

Why People Might Not Support Your Dreams:

Fear for your safety: They genuinely care about you and are worried about you getting hurt.

Projection of their own fears: Your dreams trigger their own fears about taking risks or making changes.

Comfort with the status quo: Your growth might disrupt the dynamic they're comfortable with.

Lack of vision: They can't see what you see or understand what you understand about your potential.

Scarcity mindset: They believe there's not enough success to go around, so your win feels like their loss.

Past disappointments: They've been hurt by their own failed dreams and are trying to protect you from similar pain.

How to Handle Lack of Support:

Don't take it personally: Their reaction is about them, not about you or your dreams.

Seek support elsewhere: Find people who believe in you and understand your vision.

Set boundaries: You don't have to discuss your dreams with people who consistently discourage you.

Stay connected to your why: When others don't support you, reconnect with your deeper motivation.

Prove them wrong with results: Sometimes the best response to doubt is demonstration.

Remember that you don't need everyone's support: You just need enough support to keep going.

Giving Yourself Permission: A Step-by-Step Process

If you've been waiting for permission for a while, it might feel scary to suddenly give it to yourself. Here's a process to help you transition from permission-seeking to self-authorization:

Step 1: Identify What You're Waiting for Permission to Do

Be specific. What dream, goal, or change have you been putting off because you're waiting for approval?

Step 2: Identify Who You're Waiting for Permission From

Who needs to give you the green light? Your parents? Your spouse? Your boss? Society? Make this explicit.

Step 3: Ask Why Their Permission Matters to You

What are you afraid will happen if you proceed without their approval? What do you hope their permission will give you?

Step 4: Consider the Likelihood of Getting Permission

Honestly assess: how likely is it that this person will give you the enthusiastic permission you're seeking? Have they given you permission for similar things in the past?

Step 5: Evaluate the Cost of Waiting

What is waiting for permission costing you? Time, opportunities, growth, happiness, fulfillment?

Step 6: Gather Information (Not Permission)

Instead of seeking approval, seek information. What do you need to know to make an informed decision?

Step 7: Make the Decision

Based on your values, your circumstances, and the information you've gathered, decide. Give yourself permission.

Step 8: Create a Plan

Now that you've decided, create a plan for moving forward. What are your next steps?

Step 9: Communicate Your Decision

Instead of asking for permission, communicate your decision to the relevant people in your life. Ask for support, not approval.

Step 10: Act

Start moving forward. Action creates momentum and confidence.

The Ripple Effect of Self-Permission

When you start giving yourself permission to pursue your dreams, it doesn't just change your life, it gives others permission to do the same. You become a model of what's possible when someone decides to stop waiting and start living.

How Your Self-Permission Affects Others:

You inspire courage: When others see you pursuing your dreams despite obstacles, it gives them courage to pursue theirs.

You challenge limiting beliefs: Your success challenges others' beliefs about what's possible.

You create new normals: Your choices expand what's considered acceptable or achievable in your family, community, or social circle.

You attract like-minded people: When you live authentically, you attract others who are also committed to authentic living.

You model self-advocacy: You show others what it looks like to advocate for yourself and your dreams.

Your Permission Slip

Consider this chapter your official permission slip. Permission to:

- Dream bigger than what others think is appropriate
- Take risks that make others uncomfortable
- Disappoint people in service of your authentic self
- Change your mind about what you want from life
- Succeed beyond others' expectations
- Fail and try again
- Take up space
- Have needs and express them
- Put yourself first sometimes
- Be imperfect while pursuing excellence
- Start before you're ready
- Learn as you go
- Trust your instincts
- Create your own path
- Define success for yourself
- Live your life on your terms

This permission is valid regardless of your age, background, education, experience, or circumstances. It doesn't expire. It can't be revoked by others. It's yours to use whenever you're ready.

You Are Authorized

You have been authorized to live your life. You've been authorized since the day you were born. The authorization doesn't come from outside you, but from the fact that this is your life to live. You don't need permission to be who you are. You don't need approval to want what you want. You don't need validation to pursue what matters to you.

You are the CEO of your own existence. You are the author of your own story. You are the expert on your own life. The permission you've been waiting for? You already have it. You've always had it. The question isn't whether you have permission to pursue your dreams. The question is, what are you going to do now that you know you don't need it?

Stop waiting for permission that's never coming from people who don't have the authority to give it. Start living the life that's been waiting for you to claim it.

Your dreams don't need permission.

They just need you.

CHAPTER 13: FAILURE IS NOT A FINAL DESTINATION

Failure is not the opposite of success. It's not the end of your story. It's not proof that you're not cut out for your dreams. It's not a judgment on your character, your worth, or your potential.

Failure is data. It's education. It's redirection. It's preparation. It's the universe's way of saying, "Not this way, try that way." It's the price of admission to the life you want.

But our culture has taught us to fear failure like it's contagious, to avoid it at all costs, to see it as something shameful that should be hidden or denied. We've been conditioned to believe that failure means we should give up, that it's evidence we're not meant for whatever we were trying to achieve.

This is wrong. Dangerously, life-limitingly wrong.

This chapter is about reframing failure as a necessary part of success, not an alternative to it. It's about learning to see your mistakes as steppingstones, not roadblocks. It's about developing resilience and perseverance that turn temporary setbacks into permanent growth. Most importantly, it's about understanding that failure is not a destination, it's part of the journey.

What Failure Actually Is (And Isn't)

Let's start by getting clear on what failure actually means, because most of us have been carrying around a definition that doesn't serve us.

What Failure Is:

- **An outcome**, not an identity
- **Information** about what doesn't work
- **A learning opportunity** disguised as disappointment
- **A necessary step** in the growth process
- **Feedback** from reality about your approach
- **A redirection** toward something better
- **Evidence** that you tried something difficult

What Failure Isn't:

- **A reflection of your worth** as a person
- **Proof** that you should give up
- **A permanent condition**
- **Something to be ashamed of**
- **A reason to stop trying**
- **Evidence** that you're not meant for success

- **The end of your story**

The problem is that we've been taught to treat failure like an identity rather than an event. We say "I am a failure" instead of "I experienced a failure." We let one unsuccessful outcome define our entire sense of self instead of seeing it as one data point in a larger experiment.

The Language That Changes Everything

The words you use to describe failure shape how you experience it. Here are some reframes that can change your relationship with setbacks:

Instead of: "I failed" **Try**: "I learned what doesn't work"

Instead of: "I'm a failure" **Try**: "I'm someone who takes risks and learns from outcomes"

Instead of: "This was a disaster" **Try**: "This was expensive education"

Instead of: "I should give up" **Try**: "I need to try a different approach"

Instead of: "I'm not cut out for this" **Try**: "I haven't figured this out yet"

Instead of: "I wasted my time" **Try**: "I invested in learning"

Notice how these reframes shift failure from something that happens to you to something that teaches you.

Why We Fear Failure So Much

Our fear of failure runs deep, and it's not entirely irrational. There are real reasons why failure feels so threatening:

Evolutionary Programming

Our brains are wired to avoid anything that might threaten our survival or social standing. In our ancestors' world, being rejected by the tribe could mean death. Even though failure rarely threatens our physical survival today, our brains still react as if it does.

Cultural Conditioning

We live in a culture that celebrates perfection and hides struggle. We see highlight reels on social media and think they're documentaries. We hear success stories without the failure stories that preceded them. This creates the illusion that successful people don't fail, when the truth is that they fail more often than unsuccessful people—they just don't let failure stop them.

Educational System

Most of us were educated in systems that punished failure rather than treating it as learning. Getting answers wrong meant lower grades. Making mistakes meant being corrected publicly. This taught us that failure is something to avoid rather than embrace.

Perfectionism

Many of us were raised to believe that anything less than perfect is unacceptable. This perfectionist mindset makes failure feel like a catastrophe rather than a natural part of the learning process.

Shame and Identity

We've been taught to tie our worth to our achievements. When we fail at something, we feel like we've failed as people. This makes failure feel existentially threatening.

Fear of Judgment

We worry about what others will think if we fail. We imagine that people will judge us, reject us, or see us as less capable. Often, this fear of judgment is worse than the actual failure itself.

Reframing Failure as Education

What if instead of seeing failure as the opposite of success, we saw it as expensive education? What if we treated every setback as tuition paid to the University of Life?

This reframe changes everything. When you're paying for education, you want to get your money's worth. You want to extract every lesson, every insight, every piece of wisdom from the experience. You don't waste the investment by pretending it didn't happen or by being too ashamed to apply what you learned.

The Curriculum of Failure

Failure teaches lessons that success never could:

Resilience: How to bounce back from disappointment and keep going.

Humility: That you don't have all the answers and there's always more to learn.

Empathy: What it feels like to struggle, which helps you connect with others who are struggling.

Problem-solving: How to adapt when your original plan doesn't work.

Self-knowledge: What you're really made of, what matters to you, what you're willing to endure for your dreams.

Perspective: What's truly important and what's just ego or external pressure.

Innovation: How to find new ways to approach problems when the obvious ways don't work.

Courage: That you can survive disappointment and try again.
The Hidden Gifts of Failure
Failure often brings gifts that success can't provide:

Authenticity: When you're not worried about maintaining a perfect image, you can be more genuine.

Freedom: When you've already failed, you have less to lose and more willingness to take risks.

Clarity: Failure often clarifies what you really want and what you're willing to sacrifice for it.

Stronger relationships: The people who stick with you through failure are your real friends and allies.

Inner strength: You discover reserves of strength and determination you didn't know you had.

Better judgment: Experience, including failed experience, improves your decision-making.

Compassion: For you and others who are struggling or who have struggled.

Learning from Mistakes: The Post-Failure Process

Experiencing failure is inevitable if you're doing anything meaningful with your life. But learning from failure is optional. Here's a process for extracting maximum value from your setbacks:

Step 1: Feel the Feelings

Don't rush to "learn the lesson" or "find the silver lining." First, allow yourself to feel disappointed, frustrated, sad, or whatever emotions come up. These feelings are valid and processing them is part of the growth.

Give yourself permission to:

- Be disappointed for a while
- Feel sorry for yourself (briefly)
- Grieve what you hoped would happen
- Be angry at the situation
- Feel embarrassed or ashamed (while knowing these feelings don't define you)

Set a time limit for this emotional processing—maybe a day, maybe a week, depending on the magnitude of the failure. Then move to the next step.

Step 2: Take Responsibility (Without Self-Attack)

Look honestly at your role in what happened. This isn't about beating yourself up, it's about identifying what was within your control so you can do differently next time.

Ask yourself:

- What decisions did I make that contributed to this outcome?
- What warning signs did I ignore?
- Where did I lack preparation or planning?
- What assumptions did I make that turned out to be wrong?
- How did my actions or inactions play a role?

Remember: taking responsibility is not the same as taking all the blame. Some factors were outside your control, and that's okay to acknowledge too.

Step 3: Extract the Lessons

This is where you turn your failure into education. What specifically can you learn from this experience? Consider:

- What worked well, even if the overall outcome wasn't what you wanted?
- What would you do differently if you could do it again?
- What new information do you have now that you didn't have before?
- What skills do you need to develop?
- What assumptions do you need to question?
- What warning signs should you watch for in the future?
- What resources or support do you need that you didn't have?

Write these lessons down. Make them concrete and specific.

Step 4: Look for the Redirection

Sometimes failure is the universe's way of redirecting you toward something better. Ask yourself:

- What doors might this close, and what doors might it open?
- What new possibilities does this create?
- How might this lead you to something you wouldn't have discovered otherwise?
- What does this teach you about what you really want?

- How might this be protecting you from something worse?

Step 5: Adjust Your Approach

Based on what you learned, how will you approach similar situations differently in the future? This might involve:

- Changing your strategy
- Developing new skills
- Seeking different resources or support
- Adjusting your timeline or expectations
- Modifying your goals based on new information
- Building in safeguards against the problems you encountered

Step 6: Plan Your Comeback

Failure is only final if you let it be. What's your plan for trying again, trying differently, or trying something new?

Your comeback plan might involve:

- Attempting the same goal with a different approach
- Pivoting to a related but different goal
- Taking time to develop skills or resources before trying again
- Starting with a smaller, more manageable version of your original goal
- Finding partners or mentors to help you succeed next time

Step 7: Act

The best way to process failure is to start moving toward your next attempt. This doesn't mean rushing into something without thinking, it means taking purposeful action based on what you learned. Action helps you:

- Rebuild confidence through momentum

- Apply your lessons in real situations

- Prevent rumination and dwelling on the failure

- Prove to yourself that you're not defined by one setback

The Stepping Stone Strategy

Instead of seeing failures as roadblocks, start seeing them as stepping stones. Each failure gets you closer to success by eliminating approaches that don't work and teaching you things you need to know. How Stepping Stones Work:

Each stone is necessary: You can't skip the stepping stones and jump directly to the other side. Each failure teaches you something essential for eventual success.

They're not comfortable: Stepping stones aren't meant to be places where you set up camp. They're meant to be touched briefly as you move toward your destination.

They require balance: You have to maintain your balance on each stone while preparing to step to the next one. This is the balance between learning from failure and not getting stuck in it.

They get you across: The purpose isn't to have beautiful steppingstones. It's to get to the other side. Each failure is valuable only insofar as it helps you reach your goal.

You can't see all of them from the beginning: You often can't see where all the steppingstones are until you start crossing. You have to trust that the next stone will be there when you need it.

Building Resilience: The Failure Recovery Muscle

Resilience isn't something you're born with, it's something you develop through practice. And like any muscle, it gets stronger the more you use it.

Components of Resilience:

Emotional regulation: The ability to manage your emotions without being overwhelmed by them.

Cognitive flexibility: The ability to adapt your thinking when circumstances change.

Self-efficacy: The belief that you can influence events that affect your life.

Social connection: The ability to seek and accept support from others.

Meaning-making: The ability to find purpose and meaning even in difficult experiences.

Self-compassion: The ability to treat yourself with kindness during difficult times.

Building Your Resilience:

Practice self-compassion: Talk to yourself the way you would talk to a good friend who was going through the same situation.

Develop a growth mindset: See challenges as opportunities to gain experience and grow rather than threats to your competence.

Build strong relationships: Cultivate connections with people who support you through both successes and failures.

Take care of your physical health: Exercise, sleep, and nutrition all affect your ability to bounce back from setbacks.

Develop emotional intelligence: Learn to recognize, understand, and manage your emotions effectively.

Practice mindfulness: Stay present with what's happening now rather than getting lost in regrets about the past or worries about the future.

Find meaning in adversity: Look for ways that difficult experiences contribute to your growth, wisdom, or ability to help others.

Celebrate small wins: Acknowledge progress and effort, not just final outcomes.

The Power of Perseverance

Perseverance isn't about blind persistence but intelligent persistence. It's about continuing to work toward your goals while being willing to adapt your methods based on what you learn. What Perseverance Looks Like:

Trying different approaches: When one method doesn't work, you try another rather than giving up entirely.

Learning from feedback: You adjust your approach based on results and input from others.

Maintaining long-term vision: You keep your ultimate goals in mind even when facing short-term setbacks.

Building on small progress: You recognize and build upon incremental improvements.

Getting support: You seek help, mentorship, and encouragement when you need it.

Taking care of yourself: You maintain your physical and emotional health so you can sustain effort over time.

Celebrating progress: You acknowledge how far you've come, not just how far you have to go.

When to Persevere vs. When to Pivot:

Persevere when:

- You're making progress, even if it's slow
- You're still passionate about the goal
- You're learning and growing from the challenges
- The obstacles are temporary or surmountable
- You have evidence that your approach can work

Pivot when:

- You've repeatedly tried different approaches without success
- Your goals or values have changed significantly
- The cost (financial, emotional, relational) is too high
- You have evidence that your fundamental assumptions were wrong
- New opportunities have emerged that better align with your strengths and interests

Creating Your Failure Recovery Plan

Just like you might have an emergency plan for your home or business, it's helpful to have a plan for how you'll handle failure when it happens.

Your Failure Recovery Plan Should Include:

Emotional support system: Who will you talk to when you're struggling? Who provides encouragement and perspective?

Self-care strategies: What helps you process difficult emotions? Exercise, journaling, time in nature, creative activities?

Reflection process: How will you analyze what happened and extract

CHAPTER 14: CONFIDENCE IS A PRACTICE, NOT A TRAIT

"I wish I had more confidence."

I hear this all the time. People talk about confidence like it's something you either have, or you don't, like height or eye color. They look at confident people and think, "They're so lucky. I could never be like that."

But here's what I need you to understand: confidence isn't a personality trait you're born with or without. It's not a fixed characteristic that some people get and others don't. It's not a magical quality that descends upon the chosen few.

Confidence is a practice. It's a skill you develop through repetition, like playing piano or riding a bike. It's a muscle you strengthen through consistent exercise. It's a habit you build through intentional action.

This changes everything. Because if confidence is a practice, that means you can learn it. You can develop it. You can get better at it. You don't have to wait for confidence to show up, you can create it through what you do, how you think, and how you show up in the world.

This chapter is about cultivating confidence over time through practical exercises and intentional action. It's about understanding that confidence grows not through positive thinking alone, but through evidence you prove to yourself that you're capable, worthy, and strong.

The Confidence Myth

Let's start by busting some myths about confidence that keep people stuck:

Myth #1: Confident People Don't Feel Fear or Doubt

Reality: Confident people feel fear and doubt just like everyone else. The difference is that they don't let those feelings stop them from taking action. They feel fear and do it anyway.

Myth #2: You Need to Feel Confident Before You Act

Reality: Action creates confidence, not the other way around. You build confidence by doing things despite not feeling confident, then experiencing success (or learning from failure).

Myth #3: Confidence Means Never Making Mistakes

Reality: Confident people make plenty of mistakes. They just don't let mistakes define them or stop them from trying again. They see mistakes as learning opportunities, not evidence of inadequacy.

Myth #4: Confident People Are Born That Way

Reality: While some people might seem naturally confident, most confident people have developed their confidence through practice, experience, and often through overcoming significant challenges.

Myth #5: Confidence Is About Thinking Positively

Reality: Confidence isn't about positive thinking, it's about realistic thinking, backed by evidence. It's about knowing what you're capable of because you've done it before or something similar.

Myth #6: You Either Have It or You Don't

Reality: Confidence exists on a spectrum and varies by situation. You might be confident in some areas and not others. You can build confidence gradually and specifically.

What Real Confidence Looks Like

Real confidence isn't loud or flashy. It's not about being the center of attention or never feeling nervous. Real confidence is:

Quiet assurance: Knowing what you're capable of without needing to prove it to everyone.

Willingness to be imperfect: Being okay with making mistakes because you know they don't define you.

Ability to take feedback: Being secure enough to listen to criticism and learn from it.

Comfort with uncertainty: Being able to act without guarantees because you trust your ability to figure things out.

Self-advocacy: Standing up for yourself and your needs without aggression or apology.

Boundaries: Knowing what you will and won't accept and being able to communicate that clearly.

Resilience: Bouncing back from setbacks because you know they're temporary and teachable.

Authenticity: Being yourself rather than who you think others want you to be.

Growth mindset: Believing you can develop new skills and abilities rather than thinking your capabilities are fixed.

The Confidence-Action Loop

Here's the key insight that changes everything: confidence and action create each other in a positive feedback loop.

Action creates confidence: When you do something despite feeling uncertain, and you succeed (or learn from failing), you build evidence of your capability. This evidence becomes confidence.

Confidence enables action: When you have evidence of your capability, you're more likely to take on new challenges, which creates more opportunities to build confidence.

This is why waiting to feel confident before taking action doesn't work. You have it backwards. You take action first, then confidence follows.

How the Loop Works:

1. **You take action** despite not feeling fully confident
2. **You gain experience** (successful or educational)

3. **You build evidence** of your capability to handle challenges

4. **Your confidence increases** based on this evidence

5. **You're more willing to take bigger actions** because of your increased confidence

6. **The loop continues** with each action building more confidence

Building Confidence Through Evidence

Confidence isn't built on affirmations or positive self-talk alone (though those can help). It's built on evidence—proof that you can do what you set out to do, handle what comes your way, and figure out solutions to problems.

Types of Evidence That Build Confidence:

Competence evidence: Times when you successfully completed tasks or achieved goals.

Resilience evidence: Times when you face challenges and overcame them or learned from them.

Growth evidence: Times when you developed new skills or improved existing ones.

Courage evidence: Times when you act despite feeling afraid or uncertain.

Problem-solving evidence: Times when you figure out solutions to difficult problems.

Recovery evidence: Times when you made mistakes and bounced back.

Authentic evidence: Times when you stayed true to yourself despite pressure to conform.

Creating Your Evidence Bank

Start collecting evidence of your capability by keeping track of:

Daily wins: Small accomplishments that prove your competence

Challenges overcome: Difficulties you've faced and handled.

Skills developed: New abilities you've learned

Feedback received: Positive responses from others about your work or character

Problems solved: Times when you figure out solutions

Fears faced: Situations where you acted despite being scared

Mistakes recovered from: Times when you bounced back from setbacks

Write these down. Keep a running list. Your brain is wired to notice problems and threats more than successes and strengths, so you need to consciously collect evidence of your capability.

Practical Exercises to Build Confidence

Exercise 1: The Confidence Journal

Every day for 30 days, write down three things you did that required even a small amount of confidence. These might be:

- Speaking up in a meeting
- Trying a new recipe
- Making a phone call you were avoiding
- Wearing something that made you feel good
- Setting a boundary with someone
- Learning something new

The goal is to notice that you're already acting with confidence in small ways throughout your day.

Exercise 2: The Skills Inventory

Make a comprehensive list of your skills, abilities, and knowledge. Include:

- Professional skills
- Life skills (cooking, budgeting, organizing)
- Social skills
- Creative abilities
- Problem-solving experiences
- Languages you speak
- Software you can use
- Topics you know about

This inventory reminds you of how capable you already are.

Exercise 3: The Challenge Ladder

Create a ladder of challenges in an area where you want to build confidence. Start with the smallest possible step and gradually increase the difficulty. For example, if you want to build confidence in public speaking:

1. Speak up once in a small meeting
2. Ask a question during a presentation
3. Give a toast at a small gathering
4. Present to your team at work
5. Speak at a larger meeting
6. Give a presentation to strangers

7. Speak at a conference

Complete each rung before moving to the next one.

Exercise 4: The Past Success Review

Write detailed accounts of 10 times in your life when you succeeded at something difficult or overcame a significant challenge. Include:

- What the situation was
- What obstacles you faced
- What actions you took
- What the outcome was
- What this proves about your capabilities

Read these accounts whenever you're facing a new challenge.

Exercise 5: The Comfort Zone Expansion

Once a week, do something that's slightly outside your comfort zone. It doesn't have to be dramatic—just something that requires a small stretch. Examples:

- Trying a new type of food
- Taking a different route to work
- Starting a conversation with a stranger
- Wearing a color you never wear
- Signing up for a class
- Volunteering for a project at work

The goal is to prove to yourself that you can handle new and uncertain situations.

Exercise 6: The Compliment Collection

Keep track of compliments and positive feedback you receive. Write them down, save emails, and keep notes. When you're feeling low on confidence, review this collection to remind yourself how others see your strengths and contributions.

Exercise 7: The Body Language Practice

Confidence isn't just mental. It's physical. Practice confident body language:

- Stand tall with your shoulders back
- Make eye contact when speaking and listening
- Use gestures when you talk
- Take up appropriate space
- Speak clearly and at an appropriate volume
- Walk with purpose

Research shows that changing your body language can actually change how you feel about yourself.

Exercise 8: The Preparation Ritual

Build confidence through preparation. Before challenging situations:

- Research what you need to know
- Practice what you're going to say or do
- Visualize yourself succeeding
- Prepare for potential obstacles
- Have a backup plan

Preparation reduces uncertainty, which increases confidence.

Exercise 9: The Self-Advocacy Practice

Start advocating for yourself in small ways:

- Ask for what you need
- Express your preferences
- Share your opinions
- Set boundaries
- Negotiate on your behalf
- Speak up when something isn't right

Each time you advocate for yourself successfully, you build evidence that your needs and opinions matter.

Exercise 10: The Learning Goal Setting

Set goals focused on learning rather than just achieving outcomes. For example:

- Instead of "I will get promoted," try "I will develop leadership skills"
- Instead of "I will write a bestselling book," try "I will learn how to write compelling stories"
- Instead of "I will lose 30 pounds," try "I will learn how to maintain healthy habits"

Learning goals build confidence because they're within your control and create continuous evidence of growth.

Confidence in Different Areas of Life

Remember that confidence is context-specific. You might be confident in some areas and not others, and that's normal. You can work on building confidence in specific domains:

Professional Confidence

- Develop expertise in your field
- Seek feedback and act on it
- Take on stretch assignments
- Build relationships with colleagues
- Share your ideas and opinions
- Celebrate your professional wins

Social Confidence

- Practice active listening
- Show genuine interest in others
- Share appropriate personal information
- Express your opinions respectfully
- Set social boundaries
- Engage in small talk

Physical Confidence

- Take care of your body through exercise and nutrition
- Dress in ways that make you feel good
- Practice good posture and body language
- Learn physical skills or activities
- Address health issues that affect your confidence

Creative Confidence

- Give yourself permission to create imperfectly
- Share your creative work with others
- Learn new creative skills
- Join creative communities

- Celebrate your unique perspective
- Separate your worth from others' opinions of your creativity

Relationship Confidence

- Communicate your needs clearly
- Set and maintain boundaries
- Show vulnerability appropriately
- Handle conflict constructively
- Build and maintain supportive relationships
- Practice self-compassion in relationships

Overcoming Confidence Killers

Certain thoughts and behaviors can undermine confidence. Learning to recognize and counter these confidence killers is essential:

Comparison Trap

The killer: Constantly comparing yourself to others and finding yourself lacking.

The antidote: Focus on your own progress rather than others' achievements. Remember that you're seeing their highlight reel, not their behind-the-scenes struggles.

Perfectionism

The killer: Believing you have to be perfect to be worthy or successful.

The antidote: Embrace "good enough" in most situations. Perfectionism often prevents action, which prevents confidence-building.

Catastrophic Thinking

The killer: Imagining the worst possible outcomes and treating them as likely.

The antidote: Challenge catastrophic thoughts with questions like "What's the most likely outcome?" and "How would I handle it if the worst did happen?"

Imposter Syndrome

The killer: Believing you don't deserve your success or that you'll be "found out" as a fraud. Remember that everyone feels like an imposter sometimes.

The antidote: Focus on your actual qualifications and accomplishments rather than your feelings about them.

All-or-Nothing Thinking

The killer: Believing that anything less than complete success is total failure.

The antidote: Recognize that progress comes in degrees. Partial success is still success.

Mind Reading

The killer: Assuming you know what others are thinking about you (usually negative).

The antidote: You can't read minds, and most people are too busy thinking about themselves to judge you as harshly as you think.

The Role of Self-Compassion in Confidence

Self-compassion, is crucial for building lasting confidence. When you're self-compassionate, you:

- Recover from setbacks more quickly
- Take more risks because you know you'll be okay with yourself if things don't work out
- Learn from mistakes rather than being paralyzed by them
- Maintain emotional stability during challenges
- Feel worthy of success and happiness

How to Practice Self-Compassion:

Notice your self-talk: What would you say to a friend in your situation? Say that to yourself instead.

Acknowledge common humanity: Remember that everyone struggles, makes mistakes, and has insecurities. You're not alone in your challenges.

Practice mindfulness: Notice your emotions without being overwhelmed by them. Acknowledge difficult feelings without judgment.

Treat mistakes as learning opportunities: Instead of berating yourself for errors, ask what you can learn from them.

Celebrate effort, not just outcomes: Give yourself credit for trying, even when results aren't perfect.

Confidence and Authenticity

True confidence comes from being authentically yourself, not from trying to be who you think others want you to be. When you're authentic:

- You don't waste energy maintaining a false persona
- You attract people who appreciate the real you
- You make decisions based on your values rather than others' expectations
- You feel more comfortable in your own skin
- You're less likely to be thrown by criticism because you know who you are

Building Authentic Confidence:

Identify your values: Know what matters to you and make decisions based on those values.

Acknowledge your strengths and weaknesses: Be honest about both what you're good at and what you're still learning.

Express your opinions: Share what you think, even when it's different from others' views.

Set boundaries: Protect your time, energy, and values.

Pursue your interests: Engage in activities that genuinely interest you, not just what you think will impress others.

Be vulnerable appropriately: Share your struggles and uncertainties with people you trust.

Maintaining Confidence Through Challenges

Confidence isn't a steady state, it fluctuates based on circumstances, experiences, and even your physical and emotional well-being. Learning to maintain confidence through challenges is key to long-term success.

Strategies for Maintaining Confidence:

Remember past successes: When facing new challenges, remind yourself of previous times you've overcome difficulties.

Focus on what you can control: Direct your energy toward actions you can take rather than worrying about outcomes you can't control.

Maintain your support system: Stay connected with people who believe in you and remind you of your strengths.

Take care of your physical health: Exercise, sleep, and nutrition all affect your mental state and confidence levels.

Practice stress management: Develop healthy ways to cope with pressure and uncertainty.

Keep learning: Continuously developing new skills and knowledge builds confidence in your ability to adapt and grow.

Celebrate small wins: Acknowledge progress and effort, not just major achievements.

Confidence as a Gift to Others

When you're confident, you don't just benefit yourself, you create positive ripple effects for everyone around you:

- You give others permission to be confident too

- You create a more positive, energetic environment
- You're better able to support and encourage others
- You make better decisions that benefit everyone
- You model what's possible when someone believes in themselves
- You're more likely to take on leadership roles and make positive changes

This means that building your confidence isn't selfish, it's a gift you give to your family, your community, and the world.

Your Confidence Building Plan

As we wrap up this chapter, create a specific plan for building confidence in the areas that matter most to you:

Step 1: Choose Your Focus Area

Pick one area where you most want to build confidence. Don't try to work on everything at once.

Step 2: Assess Your Current Evidence

What evidence do you already have of your capability in this area? Write it down.

Step 3: Identify Confidence-Building Actions

What specific actions could you take to build more evidence of your capability? Create a list of possibilities.

Step 4: Create Your Challenge Ladder

Organize your confidence-building actions from least to most challenging. Start with the easiest and work your way up.

Step 5: Commit to Daily Practice

Choose one small confidence-building action you can take every day for the next 30 days.

Step 6: Track Your Progress

Keep a record of your confidence-building actions and how they make you feel. Notice patterns and celebrate progress.

Step 7: Review and Adjust

Every week, review your progress and adjust your approach based on what you're learning.

Confidence Is Waiting for You

Confidence isn't something that happens to you, it's something you create through your choices, your actions, and your commitment to growth. It's not a trait you're born with or without; it's a practice you can develop starting today.

You don't have to wait until you feel confident to start living confidently. You start living confidently, and the feeling follows. Every time you take action despite uncertainty, you're practicing confidence. Every time you get back up after a setback, you build confidence. Every time you stay true to yourself despite pressure to conform, you strengthen confidence.

The confident person you admire didn't start out that way. They became that way through practice, through taking action, through building evidence of their capability one small step at a time.

You can do the same thing.

Your confidence is waiting for you. Not in some future version of yourself, but in the actions you can take today. In the boundaries you can set right now. In the risks you can take this week. In the voice you can use in your next conversation.

Stop waiting for confidence to show up and start showing up confidently.

The world needs what you have to offer. And you have everything you need to offer it with confidence.

CONCLUSION: YOUR JOURNEY IS JUST BEGINNING

Here we are, at the end of this book and the beginning of your journey. I know that might sound contradictory, but it's not. Books end, but the work of becoming who you're meant to be? That work is just getting started.

If you've made it this far, you're not the same person who picked up this book. You've been exposed to new ideas, challenged to think differently, invited to see possibilities you might not have seen before. Something has shifted, even if you can't put your finger on exactly what it is.

Understand that reading about change and actually changing are two different things. Knowing what to do and doing what you know are not the same. The real work begins when you close this book and start applying what you've learned to your actual life.

This conclusion is your invitation to step into the arena of your own life and start living the truths we've explored together.

Let's take a moment to acknowledge what you've learned, because knowledge is power only when you recognize that you have it:

You know that it's never too late to start pursuing what matters to you. Age is not a disqualifier for dreams. Your timeline is your own.

You know that your past doesn't have to define your future. What happened to you is part of your story, but it's not the whole story. You get to write the next chapters.

You know that consistency beats perfection. Small, imperfect actions sustained over time create bigger changes than sporadic bursts of perfect effort.

You know that comparison is a thief. Your journey doesn't have to look like anyone else's journey. Your path is uniquely yours.

You know that feelings don't have to drive your decisions. You can feel afraid and act courageously. You can feel uncertain and move forward anyway.

You know that external validation is nice but not necessary. You don't need permission from others to pursue your dreams or live authentically.

You know that failure is information, not condemnation. Setbacks are feedback, not verdicts on your worth or potential.

You know that confidence is a practice. You don't wait to feel confident. You build confidence through action.

You know that your journey will be imperfect. The path isn't supposed to be pretty or easy. It's supposed to be yours.

You know that you have everything you need to start. Not to finish, but to start. And starting is everything.

This knowledge is yours now. It lives in you. The question is: what will you do with it?

There's a gap between what we know we should do and what we do. This gap is where most dreams go to die. It's where good intentions get buried under everyday life. It's where transformation gets postponed indefinitely.

This gap exists for everyone. Knowing about it doesn't make you immune to it, but it does help you recognize when you're stuck in it and consciously choose to bridge it.

Why the Gap Exists:

Comfort zone inertia: It's easier to stay where you are than to venture into unknown territory, even when where you are isn't making you happy.

Analysis paralysis: Sometimes we get so caught up in planning and thinking about change that we never actually make the change.

Fear of imperfection: We want to do it right, so we wait until we feel ready, which may be never.

Lack of systems: We know what we want to change but haven't created the practical systems that make change sustainable.

All-or-nothing thinking: We think we have to transform everything at once, so we never start with anything.

External pressures: Other people's needs, expectations, and demands can crowd out our own growth agenda.

Bridging the Gap:

Start before you're ready: You'll never feel completely ready. Start anyway.

Begin with the smallest possible action: What's the tiniest step you could take today toward who you want to become?

Focus on systems, not goals: Create daily practices that move you in the right direction.

Embrace imperfection: Done imperfectly is better than not done at all.

Get support: Find people who will encourage your growth and hold you accountable.

Celebrate small wins: Acknowledge progress, no matter how minor it seems.

The journey of a thousand miles begins with a single step. But which step? Where do you start when everything feels important and nothing feels urgent?

My suggestion is to start with the thing that scares you the most. Not because fear is bad, but because fear is often a compass pointing toward what matters most to you.

Option 1: Start with Self-Reflection

If you're not sure what you want to change or pursue, start with honest self-reflection:

- What parts of your life feel most out of alignment with your values?
- What have you been putting off that you know you need to address?
- If you could change one thing about your life right now, what would it be?
- What would you regret not trying if you looked back on your life in 10 years?

Option 2: Start with One Small Habit

Pick one small daily practice that aligns with who you want to become:

- Write for 10 minutes every morning
- Take a 15-minute walk after lunch
- Read for 20 minutes before bed
- Practice one act of self-care daily
- Express gratitude for three things each day

The key is to start small and be consistent. Small habits compound into big changes over time.

Option 3: Start with One Boundary

If you're feeling overwhelmed or taken advantage of, start by setting one clear boundary:

- Say no to one request that doesn't align with your priorities

- Set a specific time when you stop checking work emails
- Ask for what you need in one relationship
- Protect one hour of your week for something that matters to you

Option 4: Start with One Fear

Identify one fear that's been holding you back and take one small action despite that fear:

- Have one difficult conversation you've been avoiding
- Apply for one opportunity you don't feel qualified for
- Share one creative project you've been keeping to yourself
- Take one social risk that could lead to meaningful connection

Option 5: Start with One Dream

Pick one dream you've been postponing and take one concrete action toward it this week:

- Research one aspect of what it would take to pursue your dream
- Talk to one person who's doing something similar to what you want to do
- Sign up for one class or workshop related to your interest
- Create one small piece of the larger project you've been imagining

The Messy Middle

After you start, you're going to hit the messy middle. The initial excitement will fade. Progress will feel slow. You'll question whether you're on the right path. You'll be tempted to quit.

This is normal. This is expected. This is not a sign that you should give up, it's a sign that you're doing something real.

The messy middle is where transformation happens. It's where you develop resilience, patience, and character that make success sustainable. It's where you learn that you're stronger than you thought and that you can keep going even when you don't feel like it.

Navigating the Messy Middle:

Remember your why: Reconnect with the deeper reasons you started this journey.

Focus on progress, not perfection: Look for evidence of movement in the right direction, even if it's small.

Adjust your approach: If something isn't working, try a different method. Flexibility is not failure.

Seek support: Reach out to people who believe in you and can remind you of your strength.

Celebrate small wins: Acknowledge every bit of progress, no matter how minor.

Trust the process: Growth isn't linear. Sometimes you need to go through difficult periods to reach breakthrough moments.

Be patient with yourself: Change takes time. Be kind to yourself as you navigate the challenges.

The People Who Will Support You (And Those Who Won't)

As you start making changes in your life, you'll discover who's truly in your corner. Some people will cheer you on, offer encouragement, and celebrate your wins. Others will question your choices, express doubt about your abilities, or even try to discourage you from changing.

This isn't necessarily because they're bad people, it's often because your growth makes them uncomfortable. Your changes might:

- Challenge their own choices or lack of action
- Disrupt the dynamic they're comfortable with
- Trigger their own fears about taking risks
- Make them worry they'll lose their connection with you

Finding Your Tribe:

Look for growth-minded people: Seek out individuals who are also committed to personal development and positive change.

Value encouragement over agreement: The best supporters might not always agree with your choices, but they'll support your right to make them.

Seek out mentors: Find people who have walked similar paths and can offer guidance based on experience.

Join communities: Look for groups, online or offline, of people pursuing similar goals or values.

Be the support you want to see: Encourage others in their growth journeys, and you'll attract people who do the same for you.

Handling Unsupportive Responses:

Don't take it personally: Their reaction is about them, not about you or your dreams.

Set boundaries: You don't have to discuss your journey with people who consistently discourage you.

Stay connected to your why: When others doubt you, reconnect with your own reasons for pursuing change.

Find validation within: The most important approval is your own.

Remember that they don't have to understand: You don't need everyone to get it. You just need to get it.

The Long Game

The work of becoming who you're meant to be isn't a sprint. It's a marathon. Actually, it's more than a marathon. It's a lifestyle. It's a commitment to continuous growth, learning, and evolution throughout your life.

This means:

- You'll never "arrive" at a place where growth stops being necessary
- You'll continue to face new challenges that require new skills and perspectives
- You'll keep discovering new aspects of yourself and new possibilities for your life
- You'll need to regularly reassess your goals and dreams as you evolve
- You'll have seasons of rapid growth and seasons of quiet consolidation

Playing the Long Game:

Focus on systems over goals: Build sustainable practices that serve you over time rather than just focusing on specific outcomes.

Invest in your learning: Continuously develop new skills and expand your knowledge. The world changes rapidly, and adaptability is key.

Take care of your health: Physical, mental, and emotional well-being are the foundation that makes everything else possible.

Build strong relationships: Invest in connections with people who matter to you. Success means little without people to share it with.

Stay curious: Maintain a sense of wonder

Hey, Friend,

I can't believe we've reached the end of this journey together. When you first picked up this book, you might have wondered where this conversation would take you. You might have been skeptical about whether change was possible, whether someone like you could actually create something different. And now here we are, pages later, and I hope you can feel it. That shift, that opening, that quiet knowing that something fundamental has changed inside you.

This isn't really an ending, though. It's a commencement. A beginning. Everything we've talked about has been preparing you for what comes next. Living it.

First, I need to say something that I hope you'll really hear in your heart. I am so freaking proud of you. Not for finishing this book (though that matters too), but for being the kind of person who picks up a book like this in the first place. For being willing to look at your life and say, "Maybe there's more. Maybe I deserve better. Maybe it's not too late."

Most people don't do that. Most people stay comfortable in their discomfort, complaining about what they don't like but never actually doing anything to change it. But you? You showed up. You invested in yourself. You chose to believe that growth was possible. That takes courage, and I don't want you to underestimate that.

This book is not meant to be inspiration that you consume and then forget. This was meant to be a guide, a reference that you return to as you build the life you want.

The real work starts now. Today. With the next choice you make after you put this book down.

And I'm not going to lie to you, it's going to be hard sometimes. There will be days when you forget everything we've talked about and fall back into old patterns. There will be moments when you doubt yourself, when you want to quit, when you wonder if any of this is worth the effort.

In those moments, remember that growth isn't linear. Healing isn't linear. Building a life that matters isn't a straight line from point A to point B. It's messy and imperfect and full of detours. And that's not a bug in the system, that's a feature. That's what makes it real.

Your Toolkit for the Journey Ahead

You're not going into this empty-handed. You have tools now. You have strategies. You have a different way of thinking about yourself, your capabilities, and your possibilities.

When you feel stuck, you know how to get moving again. When you feel overwhelmed, you know how to break things down into manageable pieces. When you feel like giving up, you know how to reconnect with your why. When you feel like you need permission, you know how to give it to yourself.

When failure happens (and it will), you know how to extract the lessons and use them as steppingstones. When your confidence wavers (and it will), you know how to build it back through action. When people try to impose their limitations on your dreams (and they will), you know how to question the source and write your own story.

When you're in the thick of it, scared, not sure if you can keep going, remind yourself that:

You are not behind. You're exactly where you need to be to start from where you are. Your timeline is your own, and it's perfect for you.

You are not broken. You don't need to be fixed or changed fundamentally. You just need to become more of who you already are underneath all the fear and conditioning.

You are not alone. Everyone who has ever built something meaningful has felt scared, uncertain, and overwhelmed. The feeling doesn't disqualify you. It qualifies you.

You are enough. Right now, as you are, with what you have, you are enough to start. You don't need more credentials, more experience, more confidence. You just need to begin.

Your dreams matter. They're not silly or impractical or too late. They're the compass pointing you toward who you're meant to become.

You can do hard things. You've already done hard things. Look at your life—look at what you've survived, what you've overcome, what you've built. You have evidence of your strength. Trust it.

Your Next Right Step

I know you might be wondering, "Okay, Kae, this all sounds great, but what do I actually do next?" And I get it. Sometimes the hardest part isn't knowing what to do, it's knowing where to start.

Don't try to overhaul your entire life tomorrow. Just take the next right step. Just do the next small thing that moves you in the direction of who you want to become. The next right step doesn't have to be dramatic or life changing.

And then, after you take that step, take the next one. And then the next one. That's how journeys work, one step at a time, one choice at a time, one day at a time.

When you start setting boundaries, the people around you will start examining their own. When you start pursuing your dreams despite fear, others will start believing their dreams are possible too.

You think you're just changing your own life, but you're changing the world. One conversation, one boundary, one dream at a time.

If you keep showing up for yourself, you will create something beautiful. It might not look exactly like what you imagined, but it will be yours. And it will be worth every bit of effort you put into it.

As we close this conversation, I want you to know that I'm cheering you on. I'm celebrating every small step you take, every boundary you set, every time you choose yourself, every moment you decide to keep going despite fear.

You picked up this book for a reason. Maybe you were feeling stuck, maybe you were ready for change, or just had a sense that there was more available to you than what you were currently experiencing. Trust that instinct. It was right.

Your life is not an accident. Your dreams are not coincidental. The calling you feel to grow, to change, to become more is not random. That's your soul telling you that you're ready for the next chapter.

The world needs what you have to offer. It needs your unique gifts, your perspective, your contribution. It needs you to become fully who you're meant to be.

You've got this. I believe in you completely, and I can't wait to see the incredible things you create.

Now, go build that life. The one that's been waiting for you to claim it.

With love and faith for your journey,
Kae R. Nelson

PS Remember that this book isn't going anywhere. Come back to it when you need a reminder, when you're feeling stuck, when you need to reconnect with your why. These words will be here, ready to support you whenever you need them. You're not walking this path alone.

ACKNOWLEDGEMENTS

To every service member who walked beside me during my time in uniform, know this book carries your fingerprints. To those who stood watch in the dark, who missed birthdays, anniversaries, and first steps…who learned to sleep lightly and carry heavy burdens quietly. I see you. I will bring you with me. To the Airmen who laughed with me in the calm and held the line with me in the chaos, thank you for teaching me what strength really looks like. It's not loud. It's not flashy. To the leaders who believed in me before I believed in myself, the ones who pushed me harder, expected more, and refused to let me shrink, thank you for showing me that growth is often disguised as discomfort. To the quiet mentors, the battle buddies, the supervisors who checked in after the hard days, and the friends who knew when to joke and when to just sit in silence, know you helped shape the person writing these pages. To those we lost along the way, your absence is still felt, your lessons still echo. You remind me daily that life is fragile, time is precious, and becoming who we are meant to cannot be postponed.

We will not falter.

We will not fail.

We adapt.

We overcome.

We reinvent.

This book is for you.

ABOUT THE AUTHOR

Kae R. Nelson is a disabled, retired veteran and high school English teacher living in the Nevada desert. Her military service taught her discipline. Her disability taught her resilience. Her classroom taught her that everyone has the power to rewrite their story. She wrote this book because she watched too many people sabotage themselves waiting for motivation instead of building discipline and got tired of it. She believes you don't need to be perfect to get there. You just need to show up. Every time. Without fail. She's not a guru or someone who has it all figured out. She's someone who chose to get uncomfortable, face her limiting beliefs head-on, and keep moving forward.